ThinkStoryline!©

2nd revised edition, 2013
ThinkStoryline!© All rights reserved.
www.thinkstoryline.com
© 2013 skillbuild inc. publishing, *www.skillbuild.net*
ISBN-13: 978-39523346-1-4

"If you can harness imagination and the principles of a well-told story, then you get people rising to their feet amid thunderous applause instead of yawning and ignoring you."

R. McKee (screenwriting coach)

ThinkStoryline!© How stories come about

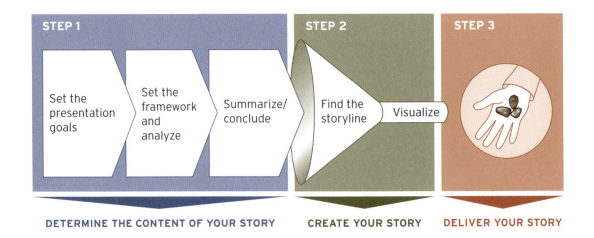

A FOLD-OUT OF *ThinkStoryline! AT A GLANCE* IS INCLUDED ON THE REAR BOOK COVER.

PREFACE - WHY *ThinkStoryline!*? WHAT'S NEW IN THE 2ND EDITION?	8
THE THREE STEPS OF *ThinkStoryline!*	10
STEP 1: DETERMINE THE CONTENT OF YOUR STORY	16
SET THE PRESENTATION GOALS	16
A. ASK YOURSELF FOUR KEY QUESTIONS	17
Question 1: What's the goal of your story?	
What's the key business question?	17
Question 2: What's in it for your audience?	21
Question 3: What's your audience's background?	
Put your audience on FIRE	22
Question 4: What key messages should your audience	
remember at 4:00 a.m.?	26
B. THE *ThinkStoryline!* PLANNING SHEET	26
KEY POINTS TO REMEMBER	30
SET THE FRAMEWORK AND ANALYZE	32
A. SET THE FRAMEWORK	34
1. Structure your business question early - it is the frame	
of your final storylined presentation	34
2. Framework options	34
a. Logic trees	35
b. Alternative frameworks	37
c. Real life examples	38
B. PRIORITIZE	40
1. Ready to take responsibility?	40
2. Establishing prioritization criteria	41
3. One-criterion prioritization (Benchmarking)	41
4. Two-criteria prioritization (2x2 matrices)	42
5. Multicriteria prioritization	43

    C. **ANALYZE TO FILL THE GAPS** — 44
        1. The hypothesis-driven approach – protecting your Achilles heel — 44
        2. How to verify or abandon the hypothesis — 47

    KEY POINTS TO REMEMBER — 49

  SUMMARIZE/CONCLUDE — 50
    A. **THE DIFFERENCE BETWEEN SUMMARY AND CONCLUSION** — 50
    B. **WHEN SUMMARY? WHEN CONCLUSION? MEANINGFUL HEADLINES** — 55

    KEY POINTS TO REMEMBER — 57

STEP 2: CREATE YOUR STORY — 58

  FIND THE STORYLINE — 58
    A. **STORIES STICK** — 59
    B. **SIX GOAL-DRIVEN TYPES OF STORIES** — 60
    C. **KEY MESSAGE FIRST? OR NOT?** — 66
    D. **HOW TO CREATE STORYLINED DOCUMENTS** — 67
        1. Pyramids as basic story structure — 68
        2. Presentation document vs. data library – make sure you and your audience make a distinction — 74
        3. From the pyramid to the story sketch — 76

    KEY POINTS TO REMEMBER — 82

  VISUALIZE YOUR STORY — 84
    A. **VISUALIZATION THROUGH YOU** — 85
    B. **TWELVE ALTERNATIVES TO POWERPOINT CHARTS** — 86
    C. **VISUALISATION WITH POWERPOINT CHARTS** — 89
        1. The message in the driving seat — 89
        2. Effective PowerPoint charts follow six rules — 92
        3. Two types of PowerPoint charts: data vs. text-driven — 94
        4. How PowerPoint's limitations can be overcome — 105

    KEY POINTS TO REMEMBER — 108

STEP 3: DELIVER YOUR STORY	**110**
DELIVER YOUR STORY	**110**
A. HOW TO TELL STORIES - THE FOUR FORMULAS	119
B. DELIVERING POWERPOINT CHARTS	121
C. FORMATS FOR THE SIX STORY TYPES	124
D. DELIVERING YOUR STORY IN E-MEETINGS	126
KEY POINTS TO REMEMBER	**128**
SOURCES OF INSPIRATION	**130**
THANK YOU	**130**
THE AUTHOR	**131**
FOLD-OUT OF *ThinkStoryline!* **AT A GLANCE**	**(REAR BOOK COVER)**

HOW TO CREATE CONVINCING PRESENTATIONS

**PREFACE – WHY *ThinkStoryline!*
WHAT'S NEW IN THE 2ND EDITION?**

When I started thinking about writing this book, one of my old music professors sprang into my mind. He explained to me that I would master a piece of music only if I could hum the melody without the score.

Data and information overload are often mentioned as the single biggest challenge in daily business life. The ability to clearly set goals and to anticipate your audience's needs proves to be more and more career relevant. How many executives and other presenters are able to deliver the melody of their presentation – or what I call the storyline – without their abundant PowerPoint chart decks?

Not knowing the storyline and the subsequent need to rely on huge amounts of PowerPoint crutches covered with font 8, is neither fun nor effective if you want to deliver messages with impact.

Lots of books have been written about different aspects of presentations. There are great books about how to design PowerPoint charts, how to solve a problem and what to do with your hands while presenting. But I haven't found any ready-to-use books including all three parts covering determining the content, creating the story and finally delivering the story. *ThinkStoryline!* closes this gap. *ThinkStoryline!* is for all who deal with presentations and love good stories.

The *ThinkStoryline!* approach tackles this issue by providing a fully integrated approach from setting the goal of your presentation or meeting, to analyzing the information, and finally, designing the story and supporting visuals needed to convince your audience.

ThinkStoryline! shows you an approach using practical story-telling tools, thought-provoking insights and ways to connect and empathize with your audience. How can you reach your audience with your presentation? Facts and logic account for fifty percent of this goal. The other half is the ability to strike your audience's emotional chords and gain their trust. I am convinced that good presenters realize that serving, inspiring and entertaining their audience is their ultimate goal.

It's about creating stories as cinematic experiences in the minds of your audience. *ThinkStoryline!* wants you to return to the great intellectual excitement of creating and telling a story.

It is amazing to just see how important stories are in our daily business life. Do you realize what impact the stories of business leaders like the wondrous Steve Jobs had? Or think of JK Rowling and her Harry Potter – she's telling a wonderful story that is not even fact based. I will demonstrate that the fairy tale of Little Red Riding Hood is a useful template for a powerful business story. As in the first edition, this new edition is designed to be a practical guide, mirror and source for reflection. It is not an academic textbook. It is strongly based on my personal experience as a consultant, trainer and coach. The tools and ideas presented in this book have proven to be helpful for a broad audience.

The first edition has generated tremendous feedback and suggestions, many of which have been included in the second edition. The chapter about creating storylined documents has been enhanced by new tools.

For example, there is a full discussion of the difference between the story being presented and the "data library". Based on my experience, the "data library", the background information containing the evidence to your story, is often mixed up with the presentation being required to achieve a specific goal in a clearly set presentation or meeting context.

Distinguishing between the storylined presentation and the data library will help you to surface the audience friendly story even more elegantly when all the data and ideas threaten to drown you.

I have also added more ideas on chart design. Perhaps most radically, I recommend banning all text charts immediately!

The section about the twelve alternatives to PowerPoint includes new tools like Prezi and some concepts of great speakers.

ThinkStoryline! has helped more than 5000 individuals around the globe so far – from automotive suppliers to zebra protectors, from University graduates to CEOs. What do they have in common? They all deal with presentations and love good stories.

You will manage your "stage fright" like a professional musician. You will tackle the score technically, create and rehearse your interpretation of all factual and nonfactual data. Connecting these dots yields your story. You are ready to perform on stage. Your story is the catchy tune of your presentation.

New York, March 2013

THE THREE STEPS OF *ThinkStoryline!*

ThinkStoryline! is an approach integrating the whole process. From setting the presentation goals, to analysis, summary and conclusion, to finding the storyline and creating the supporting visualization, and finally to delivering the story.

Let's see how this works in reality.
A car producer wants to know which set of five logos should be used to represent its new model sports car. The car company has chosen a market research agency to find out which logo is preferred by a representative group of potential customers. The key question to be answered is straightforward: Which logo is most attractive to future customers?

To answer this question, the final presentation could start as follows: "Logo No. 5 is the most promising one, based on the market research. We will demonstrate to you in the following presentation why logo No. 5 stood out."

If you have worked out the presentation goal as clearly as in the example above, your data gathering and analysis will be much more focused. Knowing the type of key message at the beginning of the project will enable you to search for the supporting story right from the start.

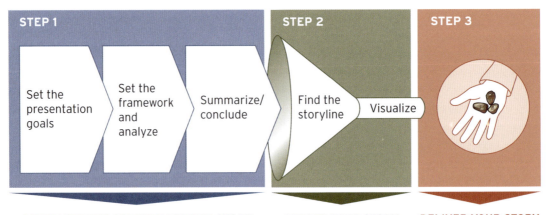

ThinkStoryline! enables you to deliver the core of your presentation even if the projector breaks down. In other words, *ThinkStoryline!* ensures that any visual aids like PowerPoint charts support you and not the other way around!

The *ThinkStoryline!* approach includes three steps:

Step 1: Determine the content of your story
Step 2: Create your story
Step 3: Deliver your story

ThinkStoryline! is applicable to all situations, especially where large sets of complex data need to be conveyed in a streamlined manner. It is useful for strategic reviews, project updates, motivational speeches or educational sessions.

I will present a number of ready-to-use tools, insights and tips, which have been successfully used by professionals in many fields who have participated in my workshops and projects.

Step 1: Determine the content of your story

"Determine the content of your story" is the first step of *ThinkStoryline!*

"Setting the presentation goal(s)" is your first task. Right from the beginning, think about what you want to achieve and what's in it for your audience. It is crucial to anticipate and decide on the amount of content your audience can absorb within a given time frame.

The tools provided in "Setting the presentation goal(s)" enable you to clearly think about different aspects of your intentions, your audience's expectations and their knowledge level. Most of the time, you already know what type of key messages will be presented in your final deliverable!

This may come as a surprise, but it is possible to think about the key messages of the final presentation during the planning phase. One example is the car-logo-testing mentioned earlier in this section. You know in advance that the key message will be which of the five proposed logos should be chosen. The second task, "Set the framework and analyze", is much less painful if you know the flavor of your key messages beforehand. You can just focus on gathering the data related to these key messages. But before you start gathering the data, take a step back and consider what the ultimate framework for your presentation should be. How can this be applied to the logo-testing project? One possible framework might be a matrix with the five logo options on the y-axis. The criteria – like "overall appeal", "positive association with speed and power", "exclusivity" – along which the logos will be evaluated would be placed on the x-axis. At this point, you already have a clear idea

■ HOW TO CREATE CONVINCING PRESENTATIONS

that you only need to gather data to fill the matrix. During the analysis, you may decide to only do a quick analysis on the less popular logos. After all, the audience are mainly interested in the winning concept. This saves the market researchers time and eliminates the detailed analysis being of no interest to the audience.

The last task within step 1, "Determine the content of your story", is to create messages by "Summarizing and concluding". The fundamental difference between summary and conclusion and their impact will be discussed. A typical end product of this activity in a business environment is a stack of PowerPoint charts, I call this the "data library".

The deadline for submitting and delivering the presentation is usually tight. *ThinkStoryline!* helps you manage these stressful conditions and will enable you to plan and storyline your presentation effectively to achieve an outstanding result.

Most presentation preparations stop after step 1. The presenter assumes that having worked out the content is enough. A (PowerPoint) bombardment might result and both presenter and audience become victims. Don't throw the entire data library at your audience!

Do you really need to show all the data you have produced and reviewed? Shouldn't you only present the essence, the answers to your audience's core questions? This saves you from struggling through loads of PowerPoint charts and data tables mostly demonstrating how much work you have done. A common misconception is that the audience should admire the presenter's knowledge and hard work rather than understanding the relevant content. That might be a reason why so many people race through 100 charts in 45 minutes. They seem to focus on justifying HOW they have come up with the results instead of WHAT the results are.

I am convinced that your goal is to show the connection between your data points. Most of the time, you are the most capable person to establish and uncover these links. Demonstrating this capability shows how intelligently you have worked rather than how hard you have worked.

That is why the next step, "Create your story", is so important and the key to achieving lasting impact.

Step 2: Create your story

You connect the dots from step 1 by creating a story. I believe "Finding the storyline" is great fun and the ultimate step to true value creation. I am convinced that highly paid professionals earn their salary by making sense of data and pieces of information rather than by wasting time on creating tables, microadjusting PowerPoint charts and realigning text boxes. Thus, a good portion of the preparation time available, say fifty percent, should be focused on creating the storyline for a presentation.

I have asked hundreds of clients to describe an ideal presentation. No one ever says that they are looking for dozens of charts and for loads of information. On the contrary, most people say they are looking for a crisp, logically flowing story with an interactive discussion that triggers insights they would not have gained by looking at the PowerPoint attachment on their own. Keep in mind that every single member of your audience wants to learn something that is new, useful and applicable.

Most of the time, the content of your presentation is logically linked in a hierarchical way like a pyramid. I will introduce the pyramid principle, a well-known and tested concept, to facilitate the process of creating the storyline. Building the pyramid will provide you with an unprecedented understanding of how the content of your presentation is interrelated. Some pieces of information may support a conclusion, which itself may be a pillar for a conclusion on a higher level again. And so on.

You can then decide whether you want to deliver your story top down by releasing the main message(s) first or whether you are going to create suspense with a bottom-up narrative as in fairy tales. The analysis of Little Red Riding Hood will illustrate what makes a story work. Our example of the market research identifying the best car brand logo is a typical example for a top-down story: "Ladies and gentlemen, our market research, covering the six most important markets in Europe, shows that logo concept No. 5 is preferred by customers. It achieved the best overall score and ranked first in three of the five categories in all researched markets. It was ranked second and fourth in the two remaining categories."

The story satisfies the primary need of your audience at a very early stage. The narrative provides them with the fact pillars about the robustness of the sample and the overwhelming supporting evidence.

"Visualize" is the last task before your presentation document is finished and ready for delivery. It may surprise you that I put "Visualize" at the end of step 2. Designing the right visuals, which greatly enhances the power of your story, is only possible after you know the actual story.

I will introduce the two basic types of charts you can create: data-driven and text-driven. I will also convince you to break the text-only chart habit.

In addition, I will suggest twelve alternatives to PowerPoint charts.

At the end of step 2, "Create your story", the dots are connected through a story and visual elements are in place to enhance the stickiness of your story. This enables you to concentrate on the delivery of your story and to keep an eye on the dynamics of your audience.

Think for a moment: How many presenters just look down at their notes or turn their backs to the audience and stare at the screen. To make things worse, they may merely read the projected PowerPoint charts out loud. These are sure-fire ways to lose your audience in a hurry!

Step 3: Deliver your story

Step 3 of *ThinkStoryline!*, "Deliver your story", provides you with tips and tricks making sure that the visuals support you as the main attraction. You will be ready for the podium to deliver the SO WHAT. Most audiences are mainly interested in the SO WHAT of a presentation. SO WHATs can be recommendations, solutions to problems or precise answers to your audience's questions. The most effective way to satisfy this need is a top-down approach by starting with the key message telling the SO WHAT. The key message can then be explained by presenting the main pillars and subpillars supporting the key message. I strongly recommend that a presentation focuses on the top messages and the supporting rationale. It encourages your audience to ask questions and helps them to fully understand the information. Answering your audience's questions helps them connect their set of dots in their story.

The top-down approach will shorten monologues and allows your audience to choose the areas they want to pursue. The top-down approach is highly relevant in business environments and particularly to a senior management audience.

The last part of *ThinkStoryline!* deals with handling situations you can't prepare for. You will face audiences asking tricky questions, displaying aggressive behavior and derailing the presentation's focus. In my experience, good stories rarely trigger this kind of hostile behavior. A good story is too exciting to be interrupted.

You have achieved your presentation goals if your audience can remember the storyline with the key messages if you call them at 4:00 a.m. the following morning!

When you reach the end of this book, I truly hope that any anxiety about creating presentations has been replaced by the excitement and pleasure of delivering good stories.

1. DETERMINE THE CONTENT OF YOUR STORY

"If you want to reach a goal, you must 'see the reaching' in your own mind before you actually arrive at your goal." *Zig Ziglar (American motivational speaker and author)*

SET THE PRESENTATION GOALS

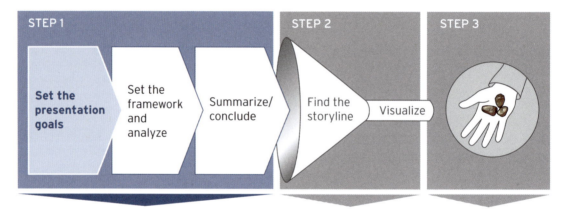

Step 1 includes three tasks: "Set the presentation goals", "Set the framework and analyze" and "Summarize / conclude".

Have you ever spent the night before a presentation in a hotel room trying to knit the data together? And have you presented red-eyed the morning after? Let's make this is a thing of the past. In this section, you will deal with the first task when applying the *ThinkStoryline!* approach: how to set the presentation goals.

That's why presentations are often lacking the all-important storylines – the presenter hasn't thougt about a storyline at all. Instead, he or she focuses on all the exciting data and findings – all the information seems important and worth sharing. You see yourself as the content expert, the "smartest kid in the room". And the unfortunate and inevitable result is being overwhelmed by the data and the impending deadline.

It's difficult not to feel overwhelmed. How can you write a crisp, clear and effective presentation if you are not fully aware of your goal and the expectations of the audience? At this point, you must stop and begin again. How can you identify and separate the valuable gold nuggets of information from the less valuable chunks? Here's how:

A. ASK YOURSELF FOUR KEY QUESTIONS

I keep asking myself and my clients four questions in an iterative manner whenever it comes to designing a presentation.

1. What's the goal of your story? What's the key business question?
2. What's in it for your audience?
3. What's your audience's background?
4. What key messages should your audience remember at 4:00 a.m.?

This forces you to take a step back before diving into the data gathering, analyzing and reviewing data stages. Applying the four questions right at the beginning of any project or presentation planning phase is crucial and highly beneficial. Your audience will follow your story naturally, feel included and embrace what you are proposing with more comfort and less doubts.

Right from the start, ask yourself these questions again and again and yet again. Work through these questions before even looking at any document, database or any other source. It is amazing what difference it makes. Most importantly, these questions will put you into your audience's mindset. The American writer John Holmes said it best: "It is well to remember that the entire population of the universe, with one trifling exception, is composed of others."

Question 1: What's the goal of your story? What's the key business question?

Try to define a successful outcome of your presentation. The outcome or goal of your presentation depends on the key business question(s) you are about to answer. It may also come in handy to have a checklist that covers the crucial elements of a solid goal. Have a look at the SMART framework:

S = Specific
M = Measurable
A = Activating, Action-oriented
R = Realistic, Relevant
T = Time-limited

It is not always necessary that your presentation goal fulfills all of the above criteria, but make sure to think about them. Most of the time though, you will find it helpful to cover them all.

Here is how the SMART approach can be employed for setting the goal of your presentation.

Specific MART

Have a look at the following example:
You are the product manager for a recently launched soft drink, SPARKLING-BUZZ. On June 26, you receive an email from your boss asking you "to provide an update on the business". You assume that this is for the semi-annual business unit conference in ten days. The email continues: **"All of our eight brands need to be discussed within four hours. The CEO will also attend."**
This brief is about as unspecific as it gets, but it sounds familiar, doesn't it? What does your boss mean? A fair assumption may be that "on the business" refers to your role in the organization.

For you, being the product manager, this could mean the sales development of SPARKLING-BUZZ in the last six months. Why six months? It is likely that this is the scope of the semiannual conference. SPARKLING-BUZZ's performance has not met expectations since its launch in January of this year. The product was expected to be the key top-line driver (less so bottom-line) of the business unit, but SPARKLING-BUZZ fell 25 percent short of the sales target by June 26. Your specific presentation goal could read as follows:
"Presenting a solution for how to recover SPARKLING-BUZZ's current budget shortfall at the half-year business unit conference (in ten days)."
Specifying the presentation goal helps you a great deal. You can focus your efforts on preparing for the presentation. And your audience know what to expect.

Be aware that the specificity of your presentation goal is fully dependent on your audience. The example of the specified SPARKLING-BUZZ semiannual update presentation illustrates this idea. While specific enough for the attendees at the semiannual conference, it would be too general for a plant manager bottling SPARKLING-BUZZ.

S **Measurable** ART

A useful presentation goal contains two kinds of measurements. Firstly, as a presenter you want to be able to assess whether your presentation has been a success. Secondly, your audience want to be able to measure whether you keep the promises you make. First and foremost, measuring is about commitment. And to carefully define what to measure is of utmost importance. Try to select criteria that are easily traceable with widely accepted indicators.

Let's assume that you have already expressed concerns about the bad sales performance of SPARKLING-BUZZ, but no one took it seriously. You decide to propose a package of short-term measures to recover as much of the budget shortfall as possible through year-end. However, the action plan may not come for free. The presentation goal now reads as follows:

"Get approval for an action plan in order to still recover as much as possible of SPARKLING-BUZZ's current budget shortfall."

Formulating the presentation goal this way enables you to assess the impact of your presentation immediately:

Did you get approval for the action plan and the budget, or not? The audience must be quite happy too: SPARKLING-BUZZ will improve its performance by December 31.

SM **Activating, Action-oriented** RT

Activating your audience is key. The contribution

An anecdote from real life shows how the success of a presentation can be measured:
A charismatic CEO had the inspiration to share his five-year strategy with his employees. He had planned 12 presentations in all parts of the country to speak to all 5000 employees. Their employees' backgrounds were very different, ranging from high school to employees with MBAs and other advanced degrees. I asked him how he would know if he had delivered the presentation successfully. He replied, "If people from all levels ask questions after my 35-minute presentation and do not immediately rush out for the free beer!"

---

of your audience is an important part of a successful presentation. And this contribution is even more significant in the meeting context.

Activate them by formulating the presentation goal as a question. This gives you a powerful opening as the audience are challenged to respond. And you pique their curiosity about how you will respond.

The "A" of SMART also stands for Action orientation, which is another powerful component of the presentation goal. It shows your audience right from the start that you have a clear plan for your presentation. Action orientation turns your presentation from reactive reporting to forward thinking problem solving.

Thus, your SPARKLING-BUZZ presentation goal has evolved:

"In order to recover most of SPARKLING-BUZZ's current budget shortfall, what actions need to be taken? Ladies and gentlemen, my presentation goal is to get your approval for the proposed action plan."

You, the product manager, are making a giant leap forward by introducing the presentation goal in this way. You started as the recipient of an update requested and you finished as a turn-around manager!

SMA **Realistic, Relevant** T

Make sure that the specificity and scope of your presentation goal are adequate for your audience (e.g., that they can take a decision or can derive personal implications). Good presentation goals are never just about information sharing. The purpose should touch the audience's emotions and be closely linked to their factual interests.

Be sure to set challenging-enough goals. If they are too difficult, you set the stage for failure. If the bar is too low, you send the message that you aren't confident or ambitious enough.

In terms of SPARKLING-BUZZ, your promise that your action plan will help to recover some of the current budget shortfall is highly relevant and hopefully realistic. If the beverages are making up 65% of the total business unit sales, and SPARKLING-BUZZ is seen as the next big bet, the CEOs in the audience will be very interested in your case. The importance of your plan might even justify nonbudgeted funds for your action plan. The most important criterion for setting a SMART goal is that you feel confident about it. If you don't, your body language will reveal it, at least subconsciously. Look at your presentation goal under this viewpoint whenever you go through the "SMARTification" process. Revise if necessary. Few people turn away from logical and exciting stories that answer relevant questions. I have the impression that the more logically your story flows, the less you will encounter picky questions, yawning, or even aggressive behavior.

I have asked many managers what they look for when attending presentations. One of the most frequent answers is that they want to see the right person is in place to make a project happen. They are less worried about the content because good managers are fully aware that they are not the content expert and need to trust their teams. This is especially true for great senior managers. In other words, every presentation is an assessment center.

Your presentation goal for SPARKLING-BUZZ needs to be minimally adjusted:

"In order to recover most of SPARKLING-BUZZ's current budget shortfall, what actions need to be taken? Ladies and gentlemen, my

goal is to get your approval for *financing* the proposed action plan."

SMAR **Time-limited**
Set a timeframe for the goal: at the end of the presentation, next week, or in three months. Putting an end-point on your goal gives you a clear deadline. It will ensure that your commitment is taken seriously. And there is no escape for you. At the same time, a fair audience take responsibility as well by implicitly granting you the time you need to make good on your promise. The product manager's completed SMART presentation goal reads as follows:
"In order to recover most of SPARKLING-BUZZ's current budget shortfall, what actions need to be taken? Ladies and gentlemen, my goal is to get your approval for financing the proposed action plan through year-end."
The original presentation goal "...to provide an update about the business..." has evolved quite a lot, hasn't it? It has become truly SMART. Let's test its robustness with the three other key questions.

Question 2: What's in it for your audience?

What presentation will you attend next? Jot down what the presenter has to deliver in order for you to consider the time well spent. You can do this mental exercise for your presentations too. Put yourself in the shoes of all the key people attending and write down what they are interested in or even what is at stake for them.

Now look at your SMART presentation goal again. If you find a mismatch between your SMART presentation goal and their motivations, finetune your presentation goal by taking into account your audience's needs.

This question has substantial consequences for you as the SPARKLING-BUZZ product manager. The presentation goal puts your boss on the spot as well. He will painfully remember that he ignored your warnings earlier in the year. What would the CEO say if he just found out about the challenges during the presentation? That would be embarrassing, wouldn't it? It might even turn the whole meeting into a destructive finger-pointing session.

Dealing with this second question allows you to anticipate potential trouble. You decide to meet with your boss. He reacts in a positive way by acknowledging your SMART work. He concedes that the sales performance has been suboptimally managed by him and the team. But he happens to be an optimist. He wants you to tell the story as an opportunity to move forward and promises you all possible support.

When I ask this second question about the audience's benefits in my workshop, participants come up with a surprisingly homogenous set of expectations. Attendees want to learn new things, follow a logically structured story, take away information that they can use immediately. They want to be entertained by an inspiring presenter. They never mention that they expect a voluminous set of PowerPoint charts. This means that presenting 50 charts in 20 minutes or reading charts out loud are no-goes. Treat your audience as sophisticated adults and make them a dynamic part of the presentation. You have presentation goals and your audience have expectations. Deliver on both.

Question 3: What's your audience's background? Put your audience on FIRE

You always strive to address your audience's needs. By answering questions one and two, you have worked on your and your audience's goals. Working through question three will allow you to identify the knowledge levels of your audience by examining each of the four "FIRE" (**F**undamentals-**I**nsights-**R**eassurance-**E**xecution) levels.

On the first level your audience will require information about the **Fundamentals** of a topic in order to gain **Insights** (level two), but still be needing **Reassurance** (level three). On this level, the needs of your audience are nonrational and also subconsciously driven. It's only when your audience have been sufficiently reassured that they will be ready to think and act on level four, **Execution**. The four **FIRE** levels help you customize the content and the flow of your story. Furthermore, the four **FIRE** levels help you to determine which of the four roles you should play as a presenter.

The first level is about familiarizing your audience with the **Fundamentals** of a topic. You will typically present a structured summary about the basic facts to educate your audience. You wear the hat of a teacher or expert. The tailored storyline will aim at providing data such as market size or competitor information. An important task is to bring the topic to life for your audience. Use concrete examples, facts, benchmarks and anecdotes. If you have managed to make your audience aware of a topic, they will typically start asking questions about your opinion, different options, implications and missing facts. They are not yet able to take it further on their own, nor are they convinced to what extent it matters to them.

So the second task is to bring your audience to the **Insights** level. Your audience will start reflecting about the fundamentals they have learned. You have reached a stage where options and implications can be analyzed. Discussions in such groups tend to be rational. But inevitably, you will hear from unenthusiastic and doubtful participants. Any pile of facts, even well wrapped in a story and logically presented, can be interpreted in various ways. Everyone in the audience has a different background and a different set of experiences. That will be reflected in the way they see the content. That's why it is important to know that your audience still perceive you as the mastermind. Forming hypotheses based on the facts and discussions and reaching agreement on a potential set of options is the best you can achieve at this stage. You are highly unlikely to get a unified view or course of action. At this stage, it is likely that you switch between the teacher and mastermind roles facilitating insight generation. The next task is to provide your audience with **Reassurance**. Promoting an audience from the second to the third level is outside the realm of PowerPoint and brilliant analysis. It is about empathy, trust, confidence and vision. At this stage

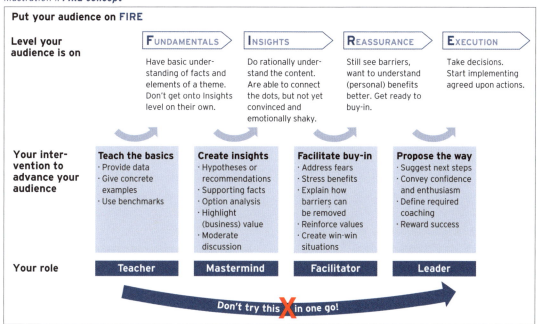

Illustration 1: *FIRE concept*

the audience integrate the information, feelings, hopes, fears and past experiences.

Your main role is to facilitate buy-in. As a facilitator, you can be of great help to craft a shared vision and to broker win-win situations. You are in the perfect position to emphasize benefits and to address fears and to suggest how barriers can be removed.

At this point, think carefully whether a formal presentation is the right format to take your audience to the level where many subconscious processes take place.

The endpoint of this stage is that your audience will embrace the goal of your presentation with both the right and the left parts of the brain. They are now ready to take decisions.

Now you must take your audience to the final stage, the **Execution** level. Their commitment to contribute to the proposed actions shows that they have understood the importance of the topic. To achieve this goal, you will need to act as a leader, displaying confidence that you will successfully execute your plan when the proposed decisions are made. Now your audience are ready to devote time, money and passion. They are also prepared to take risks. Your storyline will highlight the detailed next steps, convey confidence and enthusiasm, and show how success will be celebrated.

Now let's look at how to give presentations to non-homogenous groups. There are several strategies about how to manage this challenge because you don't want to punish all those who have a lot of knowledge of the topic.

Scenario 1: Your key decision maker is on the "Fundamentals" level, but the rest of the audience is on the "Reassurance" level. Solution: Try to see the key decision maker before the presentation. Share your points one-to-one. At the presentation, do NOT deliver a monologue. Take advantage of the other "experts" in the room by including them in the presentation and discussion.

Scenario 2: The majority of your audience is on the "Insights" level and one person is on the "Reassurance" level.

The "Insights" attendees will ask question after question. Solution: Make sure NOT to answer them yourself. By including the other "Reassured" individual, you have a powerful ally to move the "Insights only" attendees to the "Reassurance" level.

Scenario 3: The majority of your audience is firmly on the "Execution" level, but one key person is still on the "Reassurance" level. Solution: This is a good opportunity for you to step back. The only

"Reassured" forces the rest of the group to explain the action plan again. This may further clarify the situation.

The FIRE levels are also a good compass to manage your own expectations. Never try to progress more than two levels in one presentation, meeting or workshop.

This will alleviate some of the pressure you put on yourself. It will further prevent you from knocking out your audience with too much information they are not yet ready for.

The FIRE process is by no means linear. Relapses occur frequently. Do you remember a difficult project you were involved in? You may have oscillated between hectic "Execution" and "Fundamental" reassessment of the project's goals.

Back to the office of SPARKLING-BUZZ's brand team. You anticipate your audience to be partly on the Insights, partly on the Reassurance level. Hence, the goal is to move the CEO (likely to be on the Insights level) and the audience to the Execution stage.

> I have worked with a pharmaceutical company in Russia, in a very sizeable and fast growing market. The company is about to launch a major product in this market. We approached the target group, doctors from two specialties, by looking at them through the FIRE lens. The four FIRE levels enabled the company to time the messages they wanted to convey. The team decided to focus on company information and the scientific basics of the product as the best way to bring their target group to the Fundamentals level. They decided to hold off talking about the commercial component story of the drug, yet.
>
> The strategy to move the doctors forward to the Insights stage involved convincing them rationally of the major advantages of this new drug. For example, patients would benefit from increased convenience without sacrificing any efficacy or safety.
>
> However, there was one issue regarding the perceived high price of the treatment. The strategy was to tackle the Reassurance part from three angles. There were pharmaco economic models suggesting that the treatment would be worthwhile, but it required considerable time for explanation. The client also strived to provide doctors with new kinds of services. Finally, the emotional fact that convenience meant better patient compliance and less fear of the treatment was emphasized to reassure the doctors.
>
> To jump-start the Execution phase, the doctors would receive free samples of the treatment.
>
> From the selling point of view, the sales representatives were trained to determine which FIRE level the doctor is on before meeting the physician. Thus, the sales representatives could best address the doctor's needs by neither proceeding too quickly to detailed scientific data nor repeat-

ing fundamental data, which the doctor might already know from journals and congresses.

Question 4: What key messages should your audience remember at 4:00 a.m.?

Working through questions one to three establishes a robust base for building your story to a known end-point. How would you phrase the executive summary of your presentation in 15 seconds?
A rule of thumb is that implanting one message per 15 minutes of presentation with a maximum of three key messages in one presentation is realistic. By now, you and your boss have a stronger idea about improving SPARKLING-BUZZ's situation.
You can craft the first set of messages that the CEO should remember at 4:00 a.m. the following morning.
"We have a problem with SPARKLING-BUZZ, but the action plan is solid and the team can turn the situation around."
- "The nonbudgeted money needed to make the turnaround happen is spent wisely."
- "As CEO, I feel confident in announcing the turnaround of SPARKLING-BUZZ to investors at the semiannual investor meeting in 14 days. This puts me back in control."

B. THE *ThinkStoryline!* PLANNING SHEET

The next illustration introduces the *ThinkStoryline!* planning sheet. The four questions that were discussed in the last section are at its core. To complete the preparation, some logistical aspects are added as well as a section about potential hurdles and hot topics you may have to manage.
I use this sheet as a starting point for all presentations.
- **Time slot?** Make sure you know well in advance how much time you have for your presentation. A good rule of thumb is to plan two thirds of the time for delivering the "storylined" presentation. Allow the remaining one third for discussion.
- **Format?** Take a step back and ask yourself whether presenting a series of charts is the best format. There are other options:
  - Use the presentation slides as a trigger for questions. Write your audience's questions on a flip chart. This is especially useful if you have sent the chart deck to the participants in advance and if you work with a small audience. It may be quite boring for them to follow a presentation they have already read. This format rewards the ones who have read the document in advance and "punishes" those who haven't without excluding them fully.

Illustration 2: **The ThinkStoryline! planning sheet**

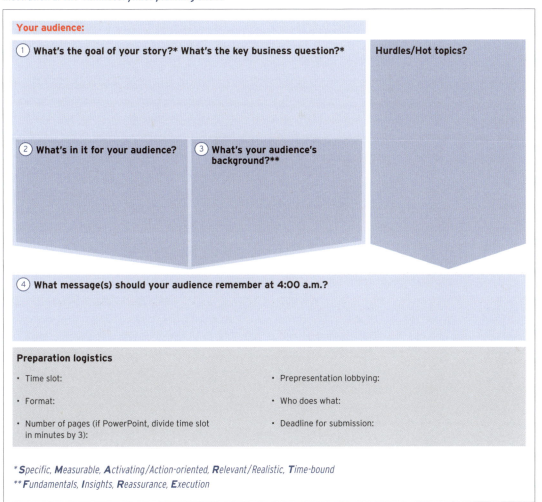

Your audience:

① What's the goal of your story?* What's the key business question?*

Hurdles/Hot topics?

② What's in it for your audience?

③ What's your audience's background?**

④ What message(s) should your audience remember at 4:00 a.m.?

Preparation logistics

- Time slot:
- Format:
- Number of pages (if PowerPoint, divide time slot in minutes by 3):
- Prepresentation lobbying:
- Who does what:
- Deadline for submission:

***S**pecific, **M**easurable, **A**ctivating/Action-oriented, **R**elevant/Realistic, **T**ime-bound
***F**undamentals, **I**nsights, **R**eassurance, **E**xecution

■ 1. DETERMINE THE CONTENT OF YOUR STORY

- Use the handout as thread while moderating the meeting for a small group instead of projecting the charts and standing the whole time. This is especially effective for advanced audiences.
- Pose at least one question: Ask your audience what their expectations are. Write them down on a flip chart at the beginning of your presentation. This gives you a good point of reference to return to at the end. You demonstrate your interest in the audience as well as your flexibility and you can measure progress and track whether the presentation has satisfied your audience.

- **Number of pages?** Divide the presentation time (in minutes) by three: Do not include title page, table of contents and tracking charts in this count. For example, if you are given a 15-minute time slot, you should aim for five content charts. This allows ten minutes (two thirds) for the presentation and five minutes (one third) for questions. The more time you spend developing your story, the less charts you will need.
- **Prepresentation lobbying?** Make sure you involve the people with something at stake. Sharing your story and obtaining their input have two advantages. You get their buy-in by taking their opinion and concerns into account for the storyline. Your audience's involvement makes them co-responsible for your presentation's successful outcome. And after all, it might help you to assess your story through your audience's eyes. I promise that this will have a clarifying effect.
- **Who does what?** The story built on key messages should simplify two important areas: delegating information gathering and focusing on required gap analyses.
- **Deadline for submission?** The material you present might not include all data. Make sure that you share required details beforehand. The usual structure of your presentation might be an executive summary, key charts and backup material to be used if needed.

Again, your audience must do the homework before attending the presentation. It rarely makes sense to mail the material just hours before the presentation. Allow at least three working days.
You see, setting the presentation goal is a crucial task. It helps to share, to think through a challenge without electronic media distraction, and to empathize with your audience in advance. Whenever possible, involve others when setting the goals.
Opposite you see the SPARKLING-BUZZ *Think-Storyline!* planning sheet.

Illustration 3: **The ThinkStoryline! planning sheet**

Your audience: The CEO and his team

① What's the goal of your story?* What's the key business question?*

"In order to recover most of SPARKLING-BUZZ's current budget shortfall, what actions need to be taken? Ladies and gentlemen, my goal is to get your approval for financing the proposed action plan through year-end."

Hurdles/Hot topics?

Management has ignored previous warnings, might be embarrassed if CEO attends

- Avoid blaming

② What's in it for your audience?

Expect solution for SPARKLING-BUZZ's sales performance issue at minimal additional investment.

③ What's your audience's background?**

SPARKLING-BUZZ is very important for entire company. Audience (incl. CEO) know fair amount about product details and promotional efforts. Audience need to advance from "Insights/Reassured" to "Execution level".

④ What message(s) should your audience remember at 4:00 a.m.?

- SPARKLING-BUZZ issue can be addressed
- The additional money will be well spent
- Confident to share SPARKLING-BUZZ action plan with investors

Preparation logistics

- Time slot: 30 minutes
- Format: PowerPoint
- Number of pages (if PowerPoint, divide time slot in minutes by 3): 10 pages
- Prepresentation lobbying: No
- Who does what: Analysts to produce updated forecast data
- Deadline for submission: In 5 days

***S**pecific, **M**easurable, **A**ctivating/Action-oriented, **R**elevant/Realistic, **T**ime-bound
***F**undamentals, **I**nsights, **R**eassurance, **E**xecution

■ 1. DETERMINE THE CONTENT OF YOUR STORY

KEY POINTS TO REMEMBER

- Investing time and applying rigor and discipline to plan your presentation will pay off in at least three ways: It enables you to focus your efforts, to serve your audience's needs and to craft an exciting story.

- Complete the *ThinkStoryline!* planning sheet making sure you cover all the important components. This activity reveals the answers to the four pivotal questions:
  1. What's the goal of your story? What's the key business question? Make it SMART (Specific, Measurable, Activating/Action-oriented, Realistic/Relevant, Time-limited)
  2. What's in it for your audience?
  3. What's your audience's background? Apply the FIRE levels (Fundamentals, Insights, Reassurance, Execution) to anticipate your audience's needs and to deliver your story in a way ensuring these needs are met.
  4. What messages of the story should your audience remember at 4:00 a.m.?

- The *ThinkStoryline!* planning sheet will become your and your team's checklist for all presentations.

- Include your audience before the start of the presentation. Ask them about their expectations and questions – this action will convert them into your allies. They share the responsibility for a successful outcome of your presentation.

1. DETERMINE THE CONTENT OF YOUR STORY

"At its heart, my work is about how to think clearly and deeply, using evidence, and all that has to pass through some presentation state." *Edward Tufte*

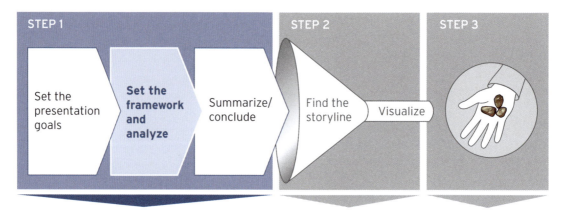

Most clients say that they have their "aha"-moments when learning about the tools and thinking about task one, "Set the presentation goals". Most of them describe their experience as putting known elements together in an integrated process step. However, almost nobody I work with has ever taken the time to structure and prioritize the goals in an explicit manner. In other words, the usually complex goals are rarely broken down into digestible pieces. The consequence is that the overview may get lost rather quickly as the presentation progresses. In the end, only a few members of the audience will still understand the full scope of the problem. This may be the second principal reason, aside from an unclear goal, for unclear data dump presentations. Imagine how helpful it will be to keep the overview and to allocate digestible tasks throughout the presentation, clearly linked to the SMART goal(s) that will ultimately lead to a clear presentation.

On the following pages, you will be introduced to a set of tools at the core of task two, "Set the framework and analyze". The aspects you will cover are "Set the framework", "Prioritizing" and "Analyzing".

Firstly, the tool kit helps to structure your initial (solution) ideas. Structuring helps you to obtain transparency about what data you already have and where the gaps remain. Establishing a structure will provide you with a framework early on in the project. This framework will "frame" your work throughout and will even come in handy as your storyline backbone for your final presentation.

Next, you prioritize the gaps by referring back to the *ThinkStoryline!* planning sheet, which you became familiar with in the previous chapter. Prioritization enables you to determine which data you need to fully analyze in more depth for proof. More generally, the end products of task two, "Set the framework and analyze", are the data and information "library" that will then be summarized and conclusions drawn. This will be the final task three of step 1, "Determining the content".

I will show you how these tools might be used to set clear goals for the market research company project: "Which of the five tested logo concepts for a new sports car model is likely to attract the most customers?"

The market researchers could set the framework by writing down the list of European countries by language. They could also note possible questions about the five logo concepts. The questions could be clustered into two categories: emotional and functional questions. The results of these frameworking efforts are two structured lists, one with the countries and one with the possible questions. Assuming that the market research project budget doesn't allow for research in all the countries, nor for the time needed for all potential questions, the market researchers suggest prioritizing the countries and questions. The six top markets account for 75% of sales in Europe. Thus, the market research company suggests doing the research in only these six countries with a group of 50 respondents in each. This group size produces statistically significant results. The research budget allows for about 15 questions for enrolling 300 participants. Shortening the list of countries by applying market potential and limiting the number of questions by using the available budget as limiting factors has enabled the market research team to prioritize according to the goal.

In the next phase, the research is carried out. All 300 participants answer 15 questions assessing the logo sketches in 5 categories. The total data set of these 300 interviews are 4500 answers requiring analysis. The analytic process focuses on distilling the most preferred logo in the group. A series of tables and graphs results. The market researchers can then summarize and draw conclusions: The data library is complete at this point. Based on this data library, the researchers can create the storyline answering which logo fares best (step 2) and deliver it (step 3) to the client.

In the next three sections, I will discuss "Set the framework", "Prioritize" and "Analyze" in more detail.

A. SET THE FRAMEWORK

Why are many presentations so hard to digest? The absence of an overarching thread holding the whole story together is one of the chief reasons. The overall framework guiding your audience through the presentation content is the result of the "Set the framework" task. This tool will greatly help you and your audience.

In terms of tools, I will focus on logic trees and briefly discuss a range of other framework devices.

1. Structure your business question early – it is the frame of your final storylined presentation

By now you have established a solid reference point for your presentation by answering the four questions needed to set the goals. Structuring the information will reveal how much you already know and how your data can be clustered. Setting the framework helps you to break down the stack heap of data into digestible pieces, and facilitate project management and communication among all stakeholders. Furthermore, framing your work will even prove very useful as your storyline backbone for your final presentation.

Keep in mind that your audience have only a limited amount of time to absorb and understand the content, either during the presentation or while reading the document beforehand. Remember, unlike you, neither will they have traveled through the entire step 1 of the *ThinkStoryline!* approach nor do they have your level of expertise.

2. Framework options

There are several useful framework options for any given presentation to reach the SMART business goal. Your framework has two purposes: it breaks down your content into manageable pieces and it provides an overarching structure that helps your audience to logically connect the information dots.

The following three sections show you two options. On page 84, in the visualization section of step 2, you can find more options for frameworks.

a. Logic trees

Logic trees start with the root of the tree being the SMART goal representing the core question to be answered by your presentation. The leaves are the potential solution ideas or answers. In the case example the leaves are the action item ideas for improving SPARKLING-BUZZ's performance, the branches are the supporting structure, linking the leaves with them to the SMART goal at the root.

When you construct a logic tree, make sure you use your SMART goal as the root. Also, think about the boundaries that could exclude some possible solutions from the beginning. For example: increasing the price of an existing pharmaceutical drug would be excluded by most companies seeking to increase revenues. Healthcare budgets are shrinking and it seems completely unrealistic to increase the price. Thus, the theoretically possible option to "increase current price" will not even be a branch of this particular logic tree.

Let's see how the product manager of SPARKLING-BUZZ has approached his challenge using the logic tree approach. Before building his tree, he assessed the impact of marketing measures used in the past. Advertising through mass and targeted channels has been very expensive and the results disappointing. Thus, he decides not to include advertising measures into his logic tree. The next illustration shows what logic tree might result for SPARKLING-BUZZ.

The SPARKLING-BUZZ logic tree

Well-constructed logic trees have four features:

1. No gaps, no overlaps. All elements contained in one branch should be similar. For example, "Increasing the price per bottle or increasing the number of bottles sold" covers all possible options. There is no other way to increase sales. You have certainly detected that the rigor tends to get looser and more practical from left to right. There are probably another 89 action ideas you could add to the existing 14 points. Be pragmatic and not overly academic. Structuring your data and thoughts with a logic tree will keep you on track and enable your audience to follow your storyline.

2. A logical flow must move along any branch of the logic tree. You can always check this by following a branch from its root to any leaf. Look at the tree on the next page to see how that

Illustration 4: **The SPARKLING-BUZZ logic tree**

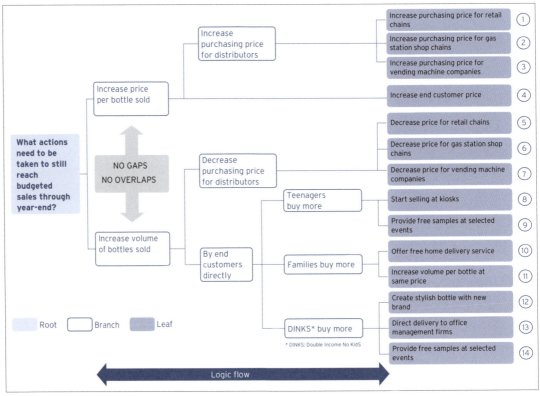

works to get to leaf number one: "In order to reach the budget, sales must be increased". One option is to "Increase the price per bottle sold". This can be achieved by "Increasing the purchasing price for distributors" and in particular "The purchasing price for retail chains". The flow also works from right to left along the branch of the tree: If we implement an "Increase of the purchasing price for retail chains", we can "Increase the purchasing price for distributors".

Hence, the price per bottle sold goes up. The result is an increase in sales in order to reach the budget. If your logic is robust, the risk of finding out that you forgot something important or created a logic flaw decreases dramatically, which in turn increases your confidence when you get on stage.

3. Be explicit by using phrases in the boxes of your logic tree – especially verbs and adjectives. Just imagine how meaningless the first leaf would become if it read like "Purchasing price for retail chains" instead of "Increase purchasing price for retail chains".
4. Avoid creating logic trees containing more than four levels. In my experience, the number of ideas just gets too big to be properly prioritized and analyzed later on. If you want to create seven levels, have a look at the presentation goal again and make sure that it is specific enough.

Like all structuring frameworks, logic trees have limitations. Logic trees are like photographs. Neither doe they represent any interaction and dependency between the branches and the leaves nor do they include a dynamic time dimension. However, logic trees provide your audience with a structured map of the solution space. Convincing them that you pruned the logic tree wisely by selecting the most relevant "leaves" of the tree will be much more transparent and less controversial when you have to justify priorities.

Logic trees result in a linear, straightforward solution finding process. Have a look at the next section dealing with frameworks that may help you to structure information that is not connected in a linear way.

> Here is a selection of possible groups for creating your logic tree that have no gaps and no overlaps:
> - Customer groups (e. g., by age, by income level)
> - Business areas (e. g., by industry, disease type)
> - Internal elements – external elements
> - Business levers (e. g., increase volume, increase price per volume)
> - Geographic (e. g., US, EU, Japan, rest of world)
> - Timing (e. g., short-term, long-term)
> - Process steps (e. g., different parts of value chain, by project phase)

b. Alternative frameworks

Frequently, your first step is data gathering. This can happen by brainstorming, by searching archives on your computer, interviewing experts or by browsing through documents. Clustering this information and setting up the pigeonholes are needed to keep the overview.

Let's return to our SPARKLING-BUZZ case. Our product manager has met with his team. They had a highly productive session and he wrote all the ideas down on post-it notes. On a flip chart, he clustered the action ideas along the value chain of his business. Have a look at the illustration on the bottom of this page.

This approach sheds a different light on his challenge. For example, the product manager could now discuss the relevant action ideas with representatives from the different departments (production, logistics, marketing, distribution). He realizes that it would be a waste of time to involve production since no sales-enhancing ideas have been identified. The downside of his value-chain based structuring approach is that he doesn't see at a glance whether these ideas include the entire realistic solution space. That is one of the advantages of the logic tree. Every structuring approach has its own pros and cons. Not *how* you set the framework, but *that* you set a framework is important. Keep in mind that a useful framework breaks down the information into digestible pieces. The ideal framework links the audience to the presentation through an already known concept (e.g., the company's value chain).

c. Real life examples

Spend enough time setting the visual frame of a presentation at the beginning of the project. In the following illustration, I have put together four examples from actual work I have done. On the left you see the context of the presentation and on the right, the framework we used throughout as thinking and storylining backbone.

*Illustration 5: **Structuring along the value chain: Increase sales of SPARKLING-BUZZ***

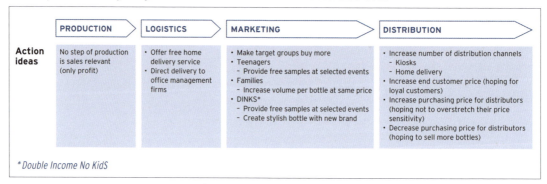

Illustration 6: **Examples of frameworks illustrating 4 different contexts**

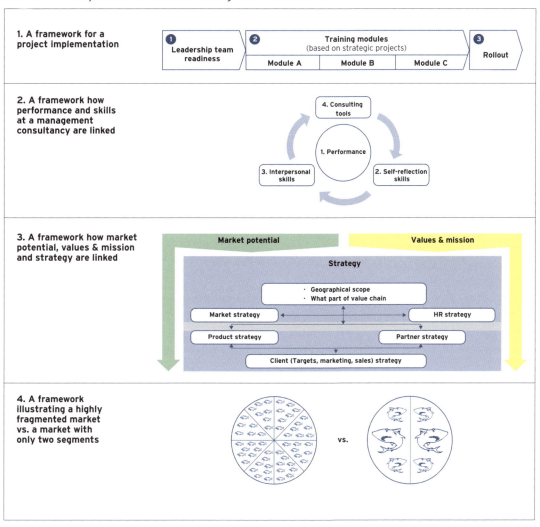

1. DETERMINE THE CONTENT OF YOUR STORY

B. PRIORITIZE

In this section, I will familiarize you with two important tools to help you prioritize your "frameworked" information.

If you have used a logic tree, prioritizing is about pruning. The thicker the branch you cut at this stage, the fewer leaves will be left to be deeply analyzed.

Prioritizing serves three purposes. It is the floodgate to protect your audience from drowning in information. At the same time, effective prioritizing creates transparency. Your audience trust you that the selection of data presented is appropriate. And that you have any additional data in your head or in a backup document if needed. Thirdly, prioritizing ensures the effective use of your time; you prevent the red-eye syndrome by avoiding unnecessary work.

1. Ready to take responsibility?

A critical point is reached. Prioritizing includes trade-off decisions, which may be taken based on hard facts and by taking softer prioritization criteria into account. It can be controversial since you make assumptions. But prioritizing proves to your audience that you are serious about serving them.

> The following list may facilitate your search for the right criteria:
> - Upside sales potential
> - Cost savings potential
> - Profitability
> - Increase in market share
> - Alignment with vision or strategy
> - Importance to audience or customers
> - Ease of implementation
> - Degree of resistance to change
> - Time (short-term vs. long-term)
> - Low risk
> - Competitive pressure
> - Market size
> - Potential to cover unmet need

Why that? Effective presentations give the audience the amount of information that is GOOD ENOUGH to make the point. Ineffective presentations flood your audience. They are driven by the fatal belief that an audience is most impressed by massive amounts of data. There is no point in showing 17 reasons why an investment makes sense if your audience are already convinced after seeing the three most powerful ones. You as the presenter have the ability and duty to select information in a purposeful way. The other 14 reasons are in the backup documentation. If you are asked for more data, present them verbally. This cements your status as the expert.

The Pareto law, also known as the 80/20 rule, suggests that 80% of a goal can be achieved with 20% of the data and analysis at hand. The big intellectual challenge is to identify which 20% you need in order to make the story good enough.

2. Establishing prioritization criteria

Take the example of the sales turnaround at SPARKLING-BUZZ. It was identified that either the price per bottle or the number of bottles sold can be increased. If it can be proved that it is unreasonable to increase prices in today's highly competitive soft-drink market, the "price branch" can be cut at this point and any price-increase related analysis becomes unnecessary. This criterion could be labeled "feasibility in this year's market environment". Defining prioritization criteria might require some time to reach agreement within a team. But this time is worth every second, as you will see in the following chapters.

I have divided the prioritization approaches by the number of criteria used.

3. One-criterion prioritization (Benchmarking)

The simplest way of prioritizing is to find a benchmark that is one-dimensional. Benchmarking is an extremely effective and powerful method of separating the wheat from the chaff. The challenge is to find a benchmark that is acceptable for everyone and applicable to all elements being assessed. Benchmarking becomes extraordinarily effective if you find a benchmark that is widely recognized. In the pharmaceutical industry, for example, a product with revenues greater than one billion USD per year is called a blockbuster.

Benchmarking can also have a simplifying effect when it is applied to presentations. Let's assume that you have to present an update on the level of awareness uptake of a public relations campaign. You ask a representative group the same 20 questions as last year. You want to show the progress made along 20 different aspects of a product. You and your team want to know which aspect to focus on. You agree to focus on the product features whose positive perception has improved less than ten percent since last year. Agreeing on that threshold of ten percent allows you to concentrate on the aspects that advanced less than ten percent.

Illustration 7: **Benchmarking**

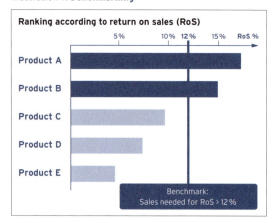

4. Two-criteria prioritization (2x2 matrices)

The next level of complexity is to deal with two prioritization criteria. I suggest using a 2x2 matrix. It is also a great instrument when you work in a team. Just put the 2x2 matrix on a flip chart, define the two criteria and work through the ideas you came up with. Your SMART goal contains several potential prioritization criteria already: the measurable aspect of your goal, the realism, the relevance and the time frame.

How can the product manager of SPARKLING-BUZZ use these criteria?

First, he revisits the presentation goal: "What actions need to be taken to reach budgeted sales for SPARKLING-BUZZ through year-end?" The natural criteria are that an action should have maximum impact on sales and be achievable through year-end. So the SMART presentation goal of his presentation also helped define the prioritization criteria.

There is one important thing to remember: Try to be as accurate as possible. Define the threshold to move from one quadrant to the next. In our case, the team decided that the impact of a prioritized action idea should have the potential to move at least ten percent closer to the budget. The second criterion is that the action idea should yield the desired results by year-end. Astonishingly, you will be able to determine where the action ideas should be placed relative to each other by roughly calculating it on "the back of an envelope". An example: It would be feasible to sell larger bottles at the same price (action idea 11). But there are two reasons why you doubt that this would yield more than a ten percent impact: You can only add 10-20 percent, otherwise you risk cannibalization. And you know that the effect of such discounts wears off quickly. According to consumer research, discounts are not the main reasons why customers switch drinks.

Sometimes you need to assess your solution ideas using more than two criteria. Putting them into a cube ("3x3 matrix") doesn't work. Your audience would be confused. But there are some elegant ways to deal with multicriteria prioritizations.

5. Multicriteria prioritization

All prioritization approaches will help you to illustrate how you reached your selection. All nonselected ideas are put aside and you can focus on the relevant ones for a specific presentation. Your audience will be appreciative as well. There are fewer balls in the air to juggle.

Some of the nonselected ones can be used in another presentation. In the SPARKLING-BUZZ case, all ideas that were deprioritized because they are

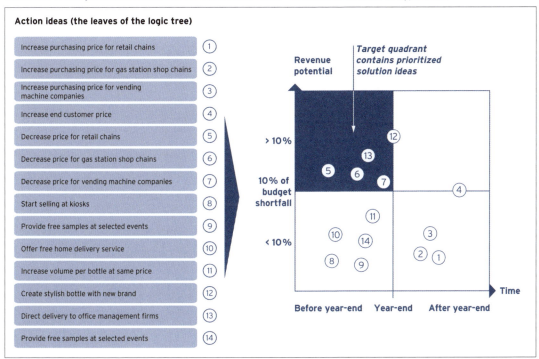

Illustration 8: *2x2 prioritization matrix for SPARKLING-BUZZ – From solution ideas to hypothesis*

not achievable until year-end, they may be reassessed for the five-year strategy.

Different approaches are necessary if you have to take more than two criteria into account. You can use a second 2x2 matrix and repeat the exercise with the elements that have been prioritized in the first matrix.

The good thing about documenting your prioritization, as shown on the next page, is that anyone looking at your presentation will be able to follow your logic. Furthermore, documentation might even help you to remember why you prioritized particular items.

One remark about why I don't recommend using scales as a metaphor. They are counterintuitive: We usually associate something higher up with winning. On a scale, however, the heavier the arguments, the lower the tray.

C. ANALYZE TO FILL THE GAPS

In this section, I will focus on filling the gaps that remain after you have structured and prioritized the existing data for your presentation.

Many books focus on the best ways to analyze data and what methodologies and tools are available.

For *ThinkStoryline!*, hypothesis-driven analysis is the most relevant concept.

1. The hypothesis-driven approach – protecting your Achilles heel

At this point, you may have an eighty percent idea of the story content. But are your argumentation, logical rigor and fact base robust enough to hold up to intense scrutiny? Where is the Achilles heel likely to be detected by your audience? How can you use the additional arguments effectively? You need them to solidify your fact base. Applying a hypothesis-driven approach is the most effective way to fill these gaps. One of the action ideas the product manager of SPARKLING-BUZZ has prioritized was the creation of a new brand for DINKS (Double Income No KidS). He knows that this is a stretch until year-end. Thus, this action idea needs thorough analysis since additional investment would be required in the short term. He remembers a great example from the pharmaceutical industry. The launch of Aspirin Cardio, a 100-mg tablet – originally a 500-mg dosage being sold for headaches – proved to be hugely successful for an entirely different patient population (blood clotting prevention). He knows from having worked on a market research project that the SPARKLING-BUZZ brand did not appeal to adults, although it received high marks for taste. As a result, SPARKLING-BUZZ was targeted to families with kids and teenagers.

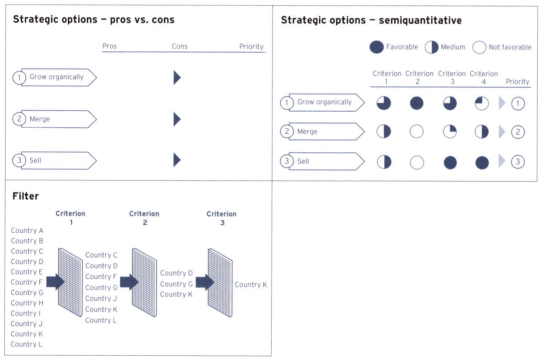

Illustration 9: **Ideas how to display multicriteria prioritization**

So far, he bases his "recommendation" on these two "facts" and the assumption that the very aggressive timing is feasible. At this stage, let's call his prioritized action idea a hypothesis.

However, he is aware of two weak points: He doesn't know the soft-drink market for adults and the potential for a new brand. Secondly: He isn't aware of his organization's budget commitment for the rest of the year. He is sure that these aspects need to be well analyzed in order to get a green light at the semi-annual meeting in ten days. He needs to perform the analyses to demonstrate whether his hypothesis is realistic from a market potential and company resource perspective. The result of these

Illustration 10: **The hypothesis-driven approach**

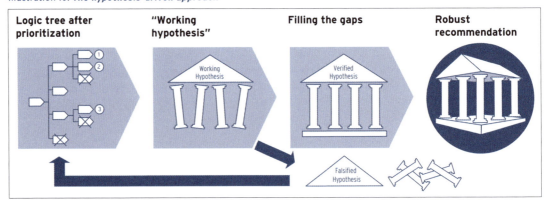

investigations will prove or disprove the hypothesis about the new brand in a fancy bottle. Indeed, filling these gaps might turn his hypothesis into a robust recommendation.

The hypothesis-based approach to analysis provides the product manager with several advantages. It will do the same for you:

- **You get the opportunity to step back.** People often tell me that being too close to the data is one of the biggest challenges they face. They feel overwhelmed by the sheer amount of data and can't see the forest for the trees anymore.

Here's how to deal with this issue: Write down what you already know (e.g., market potential, the fit with your company's product portfolio and the target customers' preferences). After that, determine what you don't know. Make sure to put yourself in your audience's shoes. What aspects are they most interested in?

- **You don't boil the ocean and you save time for creating the story.** You will be surprised about how much data you already have or know. Remember your goal is to convince your audience with an amount of facts that is GOOD ENOUGH. *This point cannot be emphasized enough!* Three supporting reasons may be sufficient, even if you could think of another

14. Make sure to develop the most convincing ones thoroughly. The others are unlikely to make it beyond the backup pages anyway.
- **You eliminate potential show stoppers early** by focusing on a few key analyses likely to validate the assumptions you made when you prioritized the data (e.g., whether five of the SPARKLING-BUZZ ideas have a greater than 10% potential through year-end).
- **You start rehearsing.** Writing down your hypothesis makes you think more specifically. You and your team become clear about what you know and what you don't. You start an inner dialogue: "What are the gaps? What questions haven't been answered?" You are much better armed if you perform this dry-run Q&A early. You still have time to fill the gaps. On stage, you don't.

2. How to verify or abandon the hypothesis

Our product manager for SPARKLING-BUZZ wants to focus on a limited amount of analyses allowing him to turn his hypothesis into a fact-based recommendation; or to abandon it before spending too much time on data crunching. The analysis sheet on the next page helped him a great deal to realize what he already knew and what gaps were left to be filled. Keep in mind that your analysis efforts stay directly linked to the overall (SMART) goal of your presentation. Hence, our manager writes down the link between the solution hypothesis and the SMART goal. He then reminds himself of what he knows already and where he anticipates gaps. He is now in a position to clearly define the analyses needed to fill his gaps. He discovers the gaps in two areas. He is unsure whether a new branded product in a fancy bottle really has such potential. And he wants to make sure that the resources needed for the launch are available. After that, our manager would have to repeat the same process for the prioritized action ideas 5, 6 & 7 (Decrease price for the three distribution channels) and action idea 13 (Direct delivery to office management firms) too.

Try this process the next time you reach this point. Develop your hypothesis from left to right.

You will see the complete picture. It will greatly facilitate the analysis process. Each member of the team will see how his or her piece of analysis contributes to the whole.

The hypothesis-driven approach to analysis will deliver crisp and powerful results in a fraction of the time it takes to boil a vast (data) ocean.

Illustration 11: **Working through a hypothesis from left to right: SPARKLING-BUZZ example**

Filling the gaps based on a working hypothesis				
Link to overall SMART goal	Working hypothesis	What you already know	The gaps	Analyses needed to fill gaps
Action idea 12: Will creating a new brand with a stylish bottle significantly improve the sales situation until year-end?	This has a potential for additional revenue (> 10 % of current budget) and will help to correct the SPARKLING-BUZZ situation by year-end	• Has worked with other consumer products • SPARKLING-BUZZ not appealing to adults (based on existing market research)	• How did they exactly do it? • Does this new brand really have such a big potential?	• Detailed case studies • Competitive intelligence of adult soft-drink market • Market research to find out perfect positioning • Business plan
	• Preparation and launch in the short term are feasible from company resource point of view	• Nothing	• How much capacity will launch of new brand absorb? • What capacity is still available based on resources already committed through year-end? • How could more capacity be made available?	• Find out from head project management • Ask business unit boss to assess potential to get resources from other products in the short term • Include additional product manager in business plan

KEY POINTS TO REMEMBER

A. Set the framework

- There is no perfect or correct framework. The information can always be structured in different ways. Each approach has limitations.

- Setting a framework simplifies the process by allowing information to be pigeonholed. It is never a perfect representation of reality.

- Your framework is useful in two ways: it dissects your content into digestible pieces and it is an overarching structure helping your audience to connect the information dots logically.

- Be pragmatic. Structuring should help you and your audience. It is not an academic exercise. Albert Einstein said: "Keep it as simple as possible but not simpler."

- The elements of the structuring approach may also be used as the table of contents for your presentation.

B. Prioritize

- Establishing and agreeing on criteria to prioritize is the first step.

- Useful criteria are applicable to both data and ideas.

- Criteria should be clear and relevant from an audience's point of view.

- Powerful tools for displaying the results of prioritizing are: benchmarking, 2x2 matrices, and multicriteria prioritization.

The result of prioritizing is a hypothesis requiring gap analysis.

C. Analyze to fill the gaps

- The hypothesis will enable you to focus and to limit the time spend on analysis.

- Documenting your gap analysis thoroughly will greatly enhance the robustness of your story and your credibility.

1. DETERMINE THE CONTENT OF YOUR STORY

"We seem as a species to be driven by a desire to make meanings; above all, we are surely homo significans – meaning-makers."

Daniel Chandler in Semiotics (1994)

SUMMARIZE / CONCLUDE

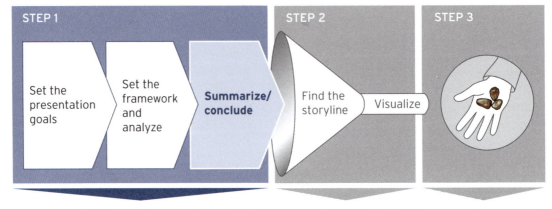

The last task of the "Determining the content" step is to understand the raw data you have accumulated and analyzed. Are they giving answers to the four key questions? In this section, you create the pieces of your story by summarizing, drawing conclusions and preparing to assemble them in step 2.

A. THE DIFFERENCE BETWEEN SUMMARY AND CONCLUSION

There are two types of statements that will eventually make up your storyline. Careful wordsmithing is required before putting them together into the storyline in the next chapter.

Look at the following statements:
Per year...
- Mauritius has 330 sunny days
- Madeira has 310 sunny days
- Bali has 318 sunny days
- Sardinia has 290 sunny days
- Maui has 322 sunny days
- Fiji has 350 sunny days

How would you summarize the above list? "Six islands averaging 320 sunny days per year" is probably the shortest summary you will find.
What about "Living on each of these islands for two months of the year would be my dream!"? Did that cross your mind as well? It is perfectly plausible to come up with that headline, isn't it? This kind of statement is very different. It is not a summary, but a conclusion based on the above facts. It includes a personal interpretation.

Some people might disagree with you. They might find your plan too boring and the temperatures in these locations too hot. They may prefer cooler locations.

In a nutshell, a summary is a shortened list of given facts whereas a conclusion brings new insights derived from given facts.

There are more fundamental differences between summaries and conclusions than meet the eye.

Illustration 12: **The difference between summary and conclusion**

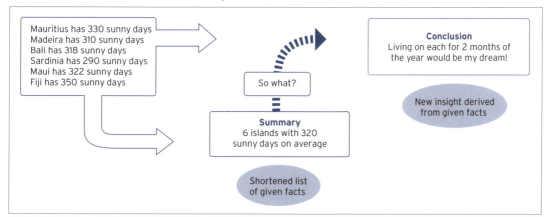

Please look at the table on the opposite page. It is a black-and-white analysis of the two types of statements. In reality, you will encounter a lot of grey areas. One way to distinguish summary from conclusion in a more sophisticated manner is to think of a summary as something white. Anything from pale grey to black is a conclusion, ranging from obvious to far-fetched.

I want to emphasize that neither a summary nor a conclusion is better or more useful. But it is important to differentiate and to decide consciously which one needs to be applied.

In theory, an unlimited number of conclusions can be drawn depending on how you look at a set of data. They will be influenced by the context and may be more or less plausible. Most importantly, they have the potential to take your audience to the next level and to add value. Think about the famous example of the half empty or half full glass: two opposite interpretations of exactly the same facts. The number of potential summaries is much smaller, since you only shorten the given facts without any interpretation. This can be very appropriate if your goal is to provide your audience with a common level of information. It is sometimes tricky to determine whether you have come up with a summary or conclusion. Here is a question to ask yourself: Could anybody potentially disagree with your statement? If yes, you have a conclusion; if no, your statement is a summary.

For example, you look for "summaries" if you want to gain an overview of different banks offering mortgages. You will then draw your conclusion by choosing the bank.

Investing your money is a different story. You expect your asset manager to make a recommendation based on his interpretation of the market and your preferences.

Both summaries and conclusions have pitfalls. Summaries can overwhelm and bore your audience. At worst, the audience might even be suspicious that you are only gathering information, but are not thinking about what they mean. Summaries of facts tend not to trigger associations or emotions and they are hard to remember.

In contrast, conclusions can be risky. They can push hot buttons. They can be wrong or your audience may not agree. They trigger emotions, body language reactions and facial expressions. Conclusions activate images and associations in your audience's mind. Conclusions are powerful and can even be dangerous. Demagogues are abusing them very consciously by painting simplistic black-and-white pictures.

Illustration 13: **Features of summaries and conclusions**

Fundamental differences between summaries and conclusions		
Differentiating questions	Summary	Conclusion
How many summaries/conclusions can be derived from a set of data?	1 – few	Many (unlimited)
Provides a neutral base for discussions?	Yes	No
Creates new insights?	No	Yes
Can take your audience to the next level?	No	Yes
Your audience might disagree?	No	Yes
Triggers your audience's emotions, launches energetic discussions?	No	Yes
The presenter might be wrong?	No	Yes
Is part of a powerful story?	Yes	Yes
May be used more if the audience do neither know you (n)or the content well?	Yes	No
May be used more if the audience know you and/or the content well?	No	Yes
Percentage of a knowledge worker's salary. How should 100% be allocated?	20%	80%

Both summaries and conclusions are part of a good presentation. The knowledge and trust level of the audience determine the ideal mix.

You have probably realized that summaries have many aspects that can be covered by inexperienced professionals and require no direct knowledge of the context. It is no surprise that numerous professional firms from low-wage countries are entering the Western markets offering market data summaries, product portfolio overviews and analyses of all kinds.

On the other hand, conclusions are less likely to become commoditized. Conclusions require much more sophisticated skills and an intimate understanding of the context. Conclusions can add tremendous insights and value. I am convinced that a knowledge worker should receive eighty percent of his or her salary for this ability.

In practice, I have worked with far too many clients – especially middle managers – who are wasting time on hectic "commodity" actions, which could be delegated or outsourced. They are often exhausted that stepping back and thinking about "what it means" doesn't happen at all. What a pity! Middle managers are in a particularly ideal position to link the raw information with the strategy. I suspect that a lot of exciting and important insights never surface.

An example illustrating this difference is shown below. On the left chart, the picture's message summarizes what the audience know already and can see without any additional statement. On the right, the chart draws a conclusion that alarms them and sets you up to deliver a convincing presentation about the proposed action plan for SPARKLING-BUZZ.

Illustration 14: **From summary to conclusion**

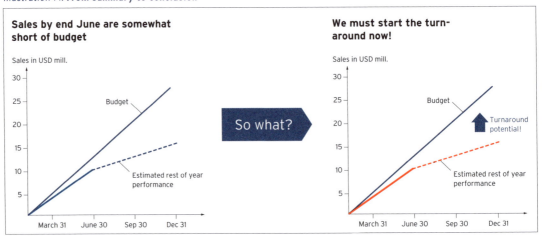

B. WHEN SUMMARY? WHEN CONCLUSION? MEANINGFUL HEADLINES

More than ninety percent of PowerPoint charts that are shown in a usual business presentation are summaries. Do you remember how many PowerPoint charts you have seen that said "overview", "market", "update (1/2)", "update (2/2)"? You may think that you will present your insights orally when you deliver the presentation. That's a fair point. But will people still be able to gain the insights if they don't attend your presentation? Many documents are sent by email only and are not delivered by the author. The second "but" is about the crispness of the language used. You will be much more precise if you have worded your summaries and conclusions in advance. Writing them down on a PowerPoint chart for example allows you to directly link the message of the chart with the content of the chart. You make optimal use of the top space of a chart.

I recommend that a good presentation contains a healthy mix of conclusions and summaries. You will lean towards summaries if your audience are on the "Fundamentals level" of the FIRE approach. Conclusions start to take over if you move your audience towards "Execution".

We have reached the end of the first step of the *ThinkStoryline!* approach. At this point the raw data is available, the analyses finished and converted into summaries and conclusions.

By summarizing and drawing conclusions, you have now prepared all the elements for your story. It's like the pieces of a puzzle laid out on a large (mental) table; in the form of PowerPoint charts, interview notes, Excel models, reports, and information in your mind. These pieces are ready to be storylined. Too frequently though, data is taken to the podium like these nonassembled pieces of a puzzle – without the story linking them. That's why I strongly recommend you to move to step 2 of *ThinkStoryline!*, "Create your story". It's time to put the puzzle!

What results did your analyses for SPARKLING-BUZZ yield? One piece of analysis was to find out the competitive situation in the soft-drink market for adults. Have a look at a part of the summary you got from the market research agency having assessed the competitive situation:

"…The soft-drink market is very dynamic and preferences are changing fast. At present, adults are looking for more premium branded beverages. We have observed that the sales for premium coffee have soared in the last years. A luxury feel around the brand is very important. This is illustrated by a recently launched Italian mineral-water brand, which offers its product in a fancy, dark blue PET bottle and seems to be doing very well…" Based on this summarized information, you as a product manager conclude that there is a good market potential for new luxury beverages.

KEY POINTS TO REMEMBER

- There is a fundamental difference between summaries and conclusions. A summary is a shortened list of given facts, a conclusion is an interpretation of a set of facts.

- Summaries provide your audience with an objective information base. They are not controversial and – if used too often – potentially boring. Conclusions can bring your audience to the next level of insights. However, they may be controversial and trigger emotions in your audience.

- Conclusions are more risky and require your audience trusting you.

- You distinguish summaries from conclusions by asking: "Could anybody potentially disagree with your statement?" If the answer is yes, you have a conclusion; if the answer is no, your statement is a summary.

- Your summaries and conclusions can be used as narrative for a presentation. Put them into the headline space of your charts.

- A good story contains a healthy mix of summaries and conclusions. You will lean towards summaries if your audience are on the "Fundamentals level" of the FIRE approach. Conclusions start to take over if you move your audience towards "Execution".

■ 1. DETERMINE THE CONTENT OF YOUR STORY

2. CREATE YOUR STORY

"The universe is made up of stories, not of atoms." *Muriel Rukeyser (American writer, 1913-1980)*

FIND THE STORYLINE

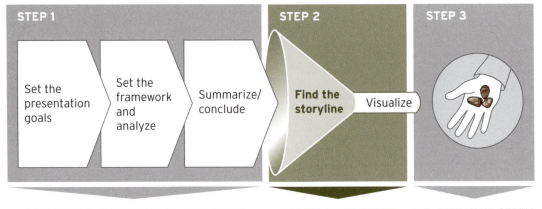

This chapter deals with the most value-creating step of the whole book: finding the storyline.
At the end of step 1 of *ThinkStoryline!*, you had determined the content and stored it in your data library. But the data library is only the future appendix of your presentation. Therefore, I strongly suggest to neither present nor send the whole library without extracting a compelling story, your presentation, from it.

Even with a SMART goal, creating your story takes time, a lot of practice and disciplined thinking.
Step 2 offers a very pragmatic approach how to create the story, complemented with ready-to-use tools. The basic concept is that your story will always support your key messages delivering on your SMART (business) goal(s).
At the end of this chapter, you will be aware of six basic types of (business) stories and under what

circumstances they might be of use. Furthermore, you will have added magic formulas to your repertoire on how to tell your stories. Parts of your brain will even be reformatted into a pyramid shape. And you will realize that the fairy tale of Little Red Riding Hood contains all the elements of an impactful business presentation.

You will achieve your goals much more seamlessly if you include "create the storyline" into your workflow. It has worked in thousands of cases so far!

A. STORIES STICK

Good stories stick because they connect the dots. Pieces of information without a story are much harder to understand and remember. As a consequence, obtaining buy-in is more difficult and decisions may be delayed.

Although you may have determined what the content should be, your audience have neither your level of expertise, nor have the audience been involved in your process of determining the content. After all, they often see the full content of your presentation for the first time when you present. We all are painfully conscious about the fact that preread materials are not very often studied carefully.

Your story serves as the vehicle transferring the content into your audience's mind. In the following sections, different approaches how the story may be structured and told are presented and discussed.

ThinkStoryline! is also a job enrichment program. Creating stories is great fun and an exciting intellectual exercise fully utilizing your brainpower. Thus, a good portion of the preparation time available for a presentation, say fifty percent, should be dedicated to creating the story. This certainly holds true for executives who are not doing the primary analysis themselves anymore.

In my experience, many executives, very senior ones included, spend far too much time on data mining and detail adjustments without seeing the overall story even if they have defined the SMART goals. Many still think that many hours of hard work and a lot of analysis and data may suffice to convince their audience.

When coaching my clients, I sometimes feel being flooded by the ingredients of a story in a random order. Who would serve his or her guests the raw ingredients directly from the refrigerator? A meal requires a careful selection of ingredients and careful cooking thereafter. Handling floods of raw information is one of our most critical challenges today. Professionals who are able to cook a compelling story from the critical information and data points have a formidable competitive edge as effective communicators paired with a less stressful lifestyle. To illustrate this, take a pen and a piece of paper. Allow 15 seconds to remember the following list of words. Cover the list after 15 seconds and write the words down.

Sea
Shoes
Boy
Pen
House
Airplane
Disc

How many of the words did you remember? All seven? How did you remember them? Empirical evidence suggests that remembering these seven words by weaving them into a story works best. Sometimes the story is quite funny though…
Try the same again. This time, create a story to remember the following list.

Stone
Guest
Kidney
Message
Garden
Table
Elephant
Music

Impressive improvements result with most groups I have worked with. The second list even had eight words.

Stories stick. I had groups where some people still remembered most of the above words half a year later by retelling the story of the guest who had kidney stones and got the message that his elephant sat on the table in his garden playing music from the Serengeti.

B. SIX GOAL-DRIVEN TYPES OF STORIES

Picasso once said, "It is hard to be young". Many of us have fond childhood memories of the moments right before it was time to go to bed. Mom and dad had to tell us a story! It seems that many of us are not aware of the power of stories anymore, at least not in the context of our professional lives.

Let's examine what elements good stories are made of. On the next two pages, I have re-written Little Red Riding Hood – the fairy tale. The second column contains a business story of a relieved manager following the threat of a hostile takeover bid. The last column illustrates the certain functional elements good stories contain regardless of their nature.

Both stories contain the fundamental **functional** elements (highlighted in bold type in the next paragraphs) of a story.

Illustration 15: **Elements of a good story**

Little Red Riding Hood – the fairy tale	A business story by Red Rock Capital's CEO	Functional element of story
Dear kids, don't be afraid; this story has a happy end.	My fellow colleagues, we have found a solution enabling our company, Red Rock Capital, to stay independent. Let me tell you how.	Answering the key question
Little Red Riding Hood was happily playing in her garden.	The market has been comfortably regulated and Red Rock Capital delivered great profits and growth.	Establishing the context, the atmosphere, introduction of the main actor(s) (Little Red Riding Hood and Red Rock Capital).
In the afternoon, her mother came up to her, limping, and said: "I am sick, but your grandmother needs her medicine. Could you cross the forest and bring it to her? Do not leave the path – there might be dangerous animals."	Up until recently, Red Rock Capital was sailing along smoothly. But then, the new EU directive put pressure on our industry and Red Rock Capital had to pay that huge fine. We are forced to alter our business into a more transparent, customer friendly one.	Introducing the task at hand. Introduction of potential sources of conflict.
Little Red Riding Hood was a good girl and took the bag with the medicine and started her journey. Half way, a wolf showed up and said: "Little Red Riding Hood, you look so nice and you are caring about your grandmother. But why not pick some flowers for her quickly to get her mind off her sickness?" Little Red Riding Hood replied: "Thank you wolf, what a great idea!" The wolf waited until Little Red Riding Hood started picking flowers and immediately went to the grandmother's house. He devoured her in one swallow, put her clothes on and waited in her bed for Little Red Riding Hood's arrival.	As you all know, we agreed with the authorities to comply and started our analysis. Some competitors approached us to do more shady deals, but we resisted and were evaluating options suiting Red Rock Capital's and our customers' purposes well. One day, The GreenStone syndicate started buying our shares secretly while we at Red Rock Capital were still peacefully strolling along towards our new future.	The main actor(s) appear(s) to manage the task with ease.

Little Red Riding Hood – the fairy tale	A business story by Red Rock Capital's CEO	Functional element of story
Little Red Riding Hood finally arrived at her grandmother's house. She started looking for her. She found her in the bedroom, but was quite surprised by her looks. She asked: "Grandmother, why do you have such big ears?" The wolf replied with a high-pitched voice disguised by chalk ingestion: "In order to hear you well!" The girl asked then: "Why do you have such big eyes?" "In order to better see you", replied the wolf greedily. Finally she asked: "Why do you have such a big mouth?" The wolf jumped out of bed and, without a word, swallowed Little Red Riding Hood in one bite.	When we had finished our evaluations, we concluded that additional capital was needed to implement our plan for Red Rock Capital's sustainable growth. We talked to many companies in our industry and also to financial investors. We invested quite a bit of time in talking and sharing a lot of information with The GreenStone syndicate. To our unpleasant surprise, The GreenStone syndicate made us aware of their hidden agenda at last and went for that public hostile takeover bid.	The showdown putting the audience on an emotional roller coaster. ↓
Fortunately, John the woodcutter passed grandmother's house and entered to say hello since he knew that she was sick. He found her in her bed, but being older and more experienced than Little Red Riding Hood, he immediately recognized the wolf's camouflage and removed the blanket. The wolf couldn't move anymore and was deeply asleep. His belly was so full! John did not hesitate. He pulled his big knife, cut open the belly and released Little Red Riding Hood and her grandmother.	In the last couple of stressful weeks, we have been talking to a lot of people within our great company. Many of them don't like the feeling of being devoured and manipulated by a pure financial investor. I am very happy to announce that we have the personal written commitment from a group of the company's managers large enough to power down The GreenStone syndicate and to finance a management buyout. We are our own white knights.	The happy end and the deserved bad end for the villain.

I chose to **address the key question of the audience** first in both stories. Telling a child that the fairy tale of Little Red Riding Hood will turn out all right may be a wise thing to do. You prevent too much anxiousness. The audience of the business presentation were similarly anxious. This audience were predominantly looking for an answer to their concern whether they would stay independent or not.

It is of paramount importance to keep the needs of your audience in mind at all times. Responding to the primary question(s) of your audience early on – e.g., addressing the main concern – is a wise choice. I have observed that presentations that satisfy the primary question(s) very early tend to be much less poisoned by detailed questions and lengthy derailments.

You may still choose to build tension in a "fairytale" like manner, with the punch line at the end. This so-called bottom-up way of story telling is effective when your audience are not familiar with the content of your story at all.

But if they are, you will enormously benefit from delivering your key message right at the beginning. An in-depth discussion of when the key message (or the "solution") should be placed first in a presentation will follow in chapter "Key message first? Or not?" (p. 66).

Let's now have a closer look at the two stories. Setting the scene by **establishing the context, the atmosphere and the arrival of the main actor(s)** (Little Red Riding Hood and Red Rock Capital in the example) lets you and your audience dive into the story right away. In a presentation, for example, this is the time to describe the business context your presentation goal is set in.

You are now ready **to introduce the task at hand.** In a presentation context, the SMART goal is the task. Typically strategic imperatives, scenarios and analyst expectations are best placed here. But when possibly challenging events appear on the scene **(introduction of potential sources of conflict)**, the audience become unsure, divided in opinion, and highly attentive.

At a first glance, the solution seems clear **and the main actors appear to manage the task with ease.**

This point **marks the showdown putting the audience and the main actors on an emotional roller coaster.**

In a presentation, this is the moment when heated discussions can flare up. If such discussions are not getting too emotional and too personal, a solution is usually found and decisions are made. The solution allows everybody to save face and moves the business task at hand into the right direction of the **happy end. The deserved bad end for the villain** should be avoided most of times in a business presentation context. Unlike in a fairy tale, the main actors of a business presentation are likely to meet their opponents again for another adventurous story where they might even serve as a good ally. It's a small world.

The functional elements we just had a look at are almost invariably present in a story. The Little Red Riding Hood pattern occurs more often in our lives than you might have been aware of: James Bond, Pretty Woman, When Harry Met Sally …

Isn't it remarkable that we go and see such stories over and over again? Even more remarkable is our desire for happy ends.

Let's now turn to an intriguing question regarding business presentations: Can we define how many different types of business stories there are?

I have identified six types based on their respective presentation goals. The six story types are also closely linked to the FIRE[1] level your audience may be on.

Here is the list of the six story types:
1. Teach – educate
2. Highlight differences (e. g., actual vs. past)
3. Create discussion platform
4. Get buy-in
5. Obtain approval
6. Call to action

The six story types cover most presentation situations you will ever face. The story concept is approached through two lenses: lens one being what goal you want to accomplish and lens two on which FIRE level your audience are.

The order of the six story types is listed according to FIRE. The following table gives you an overview on goal, FIRE level and main elements that should be included in that story type. I have also added some typical examples from daily business for which these story types may apply.

One of the most powerful features of a story is that it is easy to remember. You will be able to come up with a focused story by knowing which of these six fundamental presentation goals you are pursuing; and your audience will see a film in their heads. This is much easier and longer lasting than remembering single data points without links. An analogy from the world of music illustrates the impact: the songs with the stickiest

[1] **F**undamentals; **I**nsights; **R**eassurance; **E**xecution

Illustration 16: **The six goal-driven story types and the FIRE approach**

Story goal	Audience's FIRE level	Try to accomplish to ...	Examples
1. Teach – educate	**pre** F I R E **F** I R E	• Be highly structured • Repeat main points • Avoid overloading • Demonstrate practical use for audience	• Training courses • Introduction of new topic (e. g., market, segmentation)
2. Highlight differences	F **I** R E	• Highlight change vs. last time • Avoid repeating known facts too frequently • Reassure / create sense of urgency	• Product performance tracking • All types of updates
3. Create discussion platform	F **I R** E	• Address audience personally • Ask questions, but give no answers • Ensure interactivity • Get audience to take responsibility	• Finding solutions • Budget discussion • Difficult topics (e. g., conflict, crisis) • Creating new ideas
4. Get buy-in	F **I R** E	• Avoid providing too much structure • Use analogies • Address emotions	• Year-end speech • Overcoming resistance
5. Obtain approval	F I **R** E	• Be highly structured • Analyze pros and cons clearly • Make overall and individual benefits visible • Outline next steps and impact	• Investment plan • Strategy review • Go ahead for project
6. Call to action	F I **R** E	• Share business and emotional benefit • Describe exact next steps	• Sales presentation • Action plan

melodies make it to the top of the charts in many cases.

C. KEY MESSAGE FIRST? OR NOT?

Presenting the key message first is called the top-down approach. Top-down emphasizes the (SO) WHAT (the summary being the "WHAT" and the conclusion the "SO WHAT"). The opposite, the bottom-up approach, focuses on HOW you have come up with the (SO) WHAT. Most of us have been exposed to this second approach of telling a story so often that we got used to it. The challenge with this approach is that the presenter spends a long time on describing HOW the (SO) WHAT has been worked out. It may be too long and too complicated for your audience and concentration will fade. There are two reasons why you should be careful using the bottom-up approach. In many cases, your audience have received and read the background information already. They trust you to be the expert who knows how to do the work. Your audience are chiefly interested in the (SO) WHAT of a presentation.

Secondly, especially senior audiences want to get the key message first. Put yourself into their shoes. They are usually very busy and not too familiar with all the content details. Getting the top-line message first enables them to dig deeper where they want and to leave out details they don't need. Such an audience mainly check whether the presenter has done the homework and can be trusted. They may even perceive the bottom-up approach as being very boring.

We have conducted a piece of research proving that presenting topdown enables an audience to remember significantly more than the comparator group who had received the same presentation in a bottom-up manner. This holds especially true for longer-term memorization[2].

Does this mean the main message needs to be presented at the beginning of your presentation? YES, most of the time.

Experience shows that key messages need repetition to be remembered. Start early! You did it already by including the key messages while planning your presentation! In other words: give the answer(s) to the key business question right at the start of your presentation and present the reasons afterwards.

Have a look at the following opening of a presentation: "We have lost another 5-percent market share. Let me explain what the root causes are

[2] Presentations with an explicit outline are recalled better than ones without: A randomized controlled trial, Medical Teacher, 2010; 32: e289-e293.

and how we can stop the downward trend." This presenter assumes that the audience are mainly interested in the market share performance change. This audience would get nervous and you as presenter would get defensive, if you had shown twenty justification charts before releasing the key message of the 5-percent market share loss.

A much more successful strategy is to answer your audience's primary question first by putting on the trouble shooter's hat right at the beginning with a can-do attitude.

Illustration 17: **The six story types and key messages**

Story type	Key message first?
1. Teach – educate	No
2. Highlight actual vs. past	Yes
3. Create discussion platform	No
4. Get buy-in	Yes
5. Obtain approval	Yes
6. Call to action	Yes

Should *every* presentation start with the key message? I don't think so. The following illustration – being quite black and white – may serve you as a guide whether you ought to present your key message at the beginning.

D. HOW TO CREATE STORYLINED DOCUMENTS

Most pieces of information you want to include in your presentation are interrelated in a hierarchical way.

An example: A presenter recommends that more resources should be allocated to expand the sales force. Being in the audience, you ask yourself *why* the presenter has come up with this recommendation. One reason may be the need to match competitors who are outperforming the market with larger sales forces. Another reason may be that some regions are covered with too few sales people, and so on. These reasons support the recommendation. Hence, they are one level below the recommendation and represent the base.

Storylining is about building reasons that support the key message(s).

1. Pyramids[3] as basic story structure

A great tool helping you to visualize and understand the relationship between your key message(s) and the supporting data is the pyramid principle. There are two basic pyramid structures.

The key messages ("Switzerland is a democracy" and "HeavyRain Inc. should invest in producing more robust umbrellas") are supported by the second level in both types of pyramids. The two top levels typically form the core of a presentation. Every box on the second level may form the top of its own pyramid again. Pyramids can have multiple levels. Which type of pyramid you use depends on the nature of the content and your preference. They both do a wonderful job in structuring your story.

You will lean towards the first type of pyramid, the group structure, if your key message is based on

Illustration 18: **Two types of pyramids**

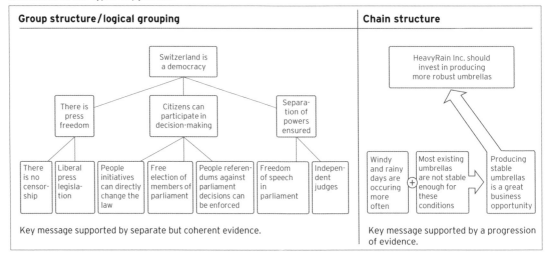

[3] The pyramid principle was invented by Barbara Minto.

separate but coherent pieces of evidence not being linked in a logical way. Typical examples are presentations where you say, "I conclude that Switzerland is a democracy. There are three main reasons." These three main reasons are then on the second level.

The second type of pyramid, the chain structure, may be appropriate when you call for "Investing in producing more robust umbrellas" at a management meeting of HeavyRain Inc. The rationale of your investment request is based on a logical progression of evidence: The starting point is that you have studied meteorological data suggesting that "windy and rainy days are occurring more often". Based on personal experience, you have found out that "most existing umbrellas are not stable enough for these conditions". Your conclusion on a general market level is that "producing more robust umbrellas is a great business opportunity". Therefore your request for "investing in producing more robust umbrellas" is standing on a solid base.

Thinking in a pyramidal way also overcomes one of the main shortcomings of the PowerPoint format: linearity. Just think about how many wormy and confusing presentations you have attended. PowerPoint's linear structure entices to present one slide after the other without highlighting or even being aware that the messages and data on the charts are not linked in a linear way. With a hierarchical structure in mind you will help yourself and your audience to pigeonhole the information and you facilitate understanding.

Let's see how the pyramid principle can be applied to the SPARKLING-BUZZ situation.

The mid-year conference is approaching and the brand manager has been working *SMARTly* to find the storyline for the SPARKLING-BUZZ challenge. The resulting "pyramidized" storyline is shown on the next page (Illustration 19).

Create dialogues between the levels

A true pyramid is made up of meaningful messages and not of generic buzzwords. In the case of the HeavyRain Inc. example, I did not put down "umbrella situation" but "Most existing umbrellas are not stable enough for these conditions". You avoid writing down buzzwords by asking "why" when you climb down in your pyramid. Say "therefore..." and you climb back up. That's how you create a dialogue between the levels. It only works with meaningful statements. Include precise adjectives and telling verbs. Have a look why "HeavyRain Inc. should invest in producing more robust umbrellas" and why "Switzerland is a democracy".

Illustration 19: ***SPARKLING-BUZZ** pyramid for a brighter future*

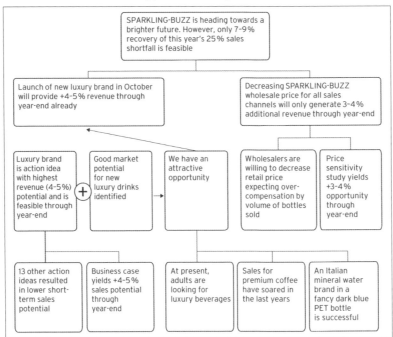

Imagine you had only put something like "weather situation" instead of "Windy and rainy days have occurred more often". The story on the second level of the HeavyRain Inc. pyramid would not work. A client once had his "Eureka moment", exclaiming, "Now I understand! I have to work with *DRAMA* words." He hit the nail right on the head. If you have a look at the pyramid about Switzerland being a democracy, the "drama" words supporting this statement on the second level are "freedom", "can participate", "ensured" (see also Illustration 20). Such words are the ingredients of an exciting story. A good way to check whether your pyramid and eventually your story

Illustration 20: **Traveling between the levels of pyramids**

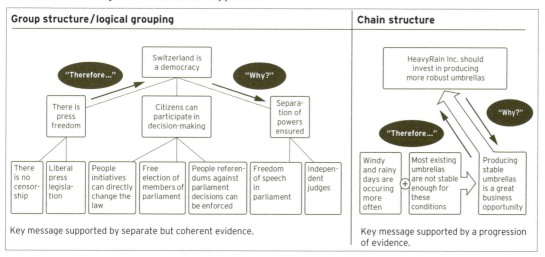

Illustration 21: **How to support every element of your key message**

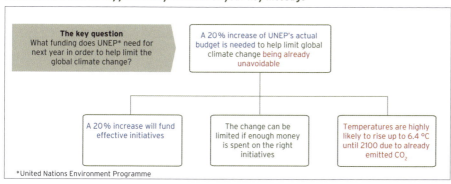

Source: ThinkStoryline!©, UNEP: Climate Change – The Current State of Knowledge (Feb 16, 2011)

are "waterproof" is to evaluate whether all parts of your key message are supported by the level below. Illustration 21 shows this. The key message consists of three elements (highlighted in blue, green and red). Each of the three boxes below supports one of these three elements.

Investing in building a pyramid before diving into the data (PowerPoint) ocean will pay off greatly in at least seven ways.

1. The key message at the top of your pyramid addresses your audience's main question right away. Your audience's primary need is satisfied right at the beginning. Through a pyramid, you can rhetorically visualize the hierarchical relationship of your story's elements.
2. Traveling up and down the pyramid using "drama words" will sharpen your logic and provide you with an in-depth rehearsal at the same time. You will know your story by heart when you get on stage.
3. The first two levels of your pyramid provide you with an option to open your presentation without charts and to signpost the main elements of your story. Later on in your presentation, you can regularly reference back to these signposts and your audience will follow your storyline easily.
4. You can address elements supporting and challenging your main message upfront and take potentially bothersome wind out of your audience's sails. An example in a chain structure: "In order to take advantage of a growing market, we should license in a diabetes compound (key message). Let me tell you why (you are climbing down to level two). The diabetes market is very large and growing. Innovative drugs could cover unmet needs and get a premium price. However, our pipeline is empty and in-licensing opportunities are costly. But we have a lot of cash. As a consequence, we are in a position to even look for expensive opportunities outside our company. Therefore (you climb back up to the top), we should license in a diabetes compound."

The story above is a mix of four supportive arguments and one challenging argument (a lot of cash may be required to license in a compound). You can deal with challenging arguments in the pyramid structure with words like despite, but, although, even, however, etc.

5. You get your executive summary by writing down the first two to three levels of the pyramid. Have a look at the "Switzerland is a democracy" executive summary:

Switzerland is a democracy
• There is press freedom
  - There is no censorship
  - Liberal press legislation

- Citizens can participate in decision-making
  - Free election of members of parliament
  - People initiatives can directly change the law
  - People referendums against parliament decisions can be enforced
- Separation of powers ensured
  - Freedom of speech in parliament
  - Independent judges

6. The first and second levels of a pyramid may serve as table of contents.

Switzerland is a democracy
1. There is press freedom
2. Citizens can participate in decision-making
3. Separation of powers ensured

That looks a bit more appealing than a generic version, which might have looked like this:

Table of contents
- Press situation
- Citizens' role
- Governmental bodies

7. A full pyramid can include many levels. It is your entire presentation at one glance. As a rule of thumb, the first two to three levels form your main presentation. The elements of the lower levels are "the library" and represent the backup documentation (see page 79).

Tip how to make your table of contents more meaningful for readers

An ordinary table of contents might look as follows:
1. Manufacturing department
2. Marketing department
3. Administration department
4. Sales department

Think about using the key message and the first level of your pyramid for the table of contents of your presentation document. Let's assume that your presentation document is about "Process cost savings potential". Have a look at the revised version of the "table of contents":

17 % of process cost savings is possible!
1. 4 % from the manufacturing department
2. 5 % from the marketing department
3. 3 % from the administration department
4. 5 % from the sales department

Tip

One challenge of sending out background material is that people usually don't read it, or only parts of it. One elegant way out is to put the top two levels of the pyramid as bulletpoints in an email. You make sure that your audience are at least exposed to the main messages before your live presentation starts.

Thinking in pyramids may also come in handy when writing clear text. Have a look at the following – spectacularly confusing – email.

"I called all airlines. They said there is no space on the flight at 5 p.m. on Tuesday, but any time from Wednesday on is ok. Flights leave every 2 hours in both directions between 7 a.m. and 7 p.m. Mr. Blackstone said he wouldn't mind moving the meeting from Tuesday to Thursday or Friday. He would then be flexible. And keep in mind that you must spend Friday with your son. Mrs. Cargil's assistant says that her boss won't be back from Vienna till late on Wednesday evening. The airport hotel gave an acceptable quote for Thursday afternoon, but it's not sure yet whether the room will be 25 sqm or 28 sqm. What do you think?"

How you can surface the essence of this email using the pyramid structure is shown in the next paragraph. It shows a distilled version of the email above.

"Reschedule the meeting to Thursday afternoon at the airport hotel.
- All three participants can attend
- Logistics are feasible and cost effective
- You can keep the promise you made to your son"

The main message is at the top of the pyramid; the three bullet points form the second level.

This email illustrates that your audience don't need to know each piece of data and is most certainly not even interested in it. "Reschedule the meeting to Thursday afternoon at the airport hotel" is all they want to know. Your value added is to analyze the data to come up with that key message and to communicate it crisply. The same thinking applies to all storylined presentations you will create from now on.

2. Presentation document vs. data library – make sure you and your audience make a distinction

Very often, you are asked to put your story into a document, most frequently into charts.

The document should be crisp, short and clear, show sufficient content depth and address your audience's needs: mission impossible? Definitely no.

You just need to look at your data from a different angle when it comes to creating documents being circulated or presented to audiences who aren't content experts and who don't need data to the greatest depth.

Usually, your audience don't have your detailed level of expertise. They are mainly interested in getting the answer(s) to their main question(s). So you need to pick the information needed to support your answers (= key messages) from your entire knowledge base, usually sitting saved as (PowerPoint) documents on your hard drive or in a data cloud. Your knowledge base – let's call it library – is usually structured following a generic structure like the alphabet. In business, this "alphabet" may sound like **Market overview, Competitor overview, Product strategy, Financials, Business risks,** etc.

Most presentations are presented following such a generic structure. Such a flow makes it very difficult for your audience to understand your reasoning that supports the key message. The reason this being so difficult is that the data supporting your key message are typically from different sections of your library. It is as if you present pages 1-50, but the information supporting your first key message are on pages 3, 17, 23, 32 and 48. As you have seen in the pyramid approach chapter, it is much easier to tell a story that shows the data from pages 3, 17, 23, 32 and 48 **grouped together under one key message.** This requires a different "storyline perspective".

It still makes a lot of sense to generate, analyze and document your data following a generic library approach like **Market overview, Competitor overview, Product strategy, Financials, Business risks,** etc. However, as soon as it comes to presenting your key messages with the supporting evidence in a succinct way, the "storyline" angle is the way to go.

Illustration 22: **From the library of facts and information to the story**

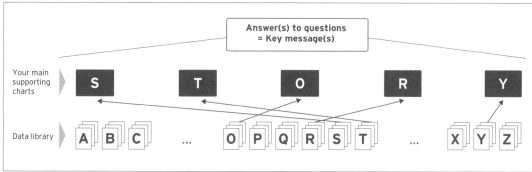

Source: ThinkStoryline!©

Illustration 22 on the previous page shows how the library links to the story and key message. The library follows the A-Z logic. For telling the "STORY" you only need "5 letters" and not in the order they occur in the alphabet. Imagine, metaphorically, I had presented my dictionary from A-Z to you. You would never have found out that I tried to tell you my STORY. You would have felt overwhelmed, bored and asking yourself "so what".

Your library becomes the backup (appendix) of your presentation document that is usually not presented in a live setting. It is the data source containing all the specific details. In this illustrative case, only the pyramid with the five supporting elements - S, T, O, R and Y - is your main presentation. It supports your key message answering your audience's questions.

3. From the pyramid to the story sketch

In this chapter, I would like to show you how your pyramid can easily be converted into a story sketch. The top two or three levels of your pyramid yield the main presentation. Everything below is in your data library and goes to the backup document. The story sketch includes the executive summary and an outline of the slides derived from it.

The executive summary: bringing key questions (your presentation goal) and answers (key messages) together

The first two levels of your pyramid are your executive summary. You have probably read or written many yourself and spent quite some time. Often, executive summaries are written at the end when all PowerPoint slides are designed already and time pressure is intense. With *ThinkStoryline!* you write the executive summary much earlier (even before you do any pretty slide!) since the pyramid provides you with the executive summary right away. The next graphic shows you how.

It may look quite different to the ones you have written so far...

First of all, the presentation goal (= key question) and the answer are shown on the same page. Most presentations I have seen contained (if at all) the goal at the beginning and the conclusions 85 pages later. On page 86, nobody will ever remember what the goals were. Even worse, the conclusions at the end of most presentations have no obvious link to the goals listed at the beginning. It seems as if the presenter had forgotten them as well.

Second, you show the core of your findings right at the beginning instead of dragging your audience through the library. Your audience get what they are looking for and you can focus on what is important to them. Illustration 23 below shows the conversion from the pyramid to an executive summary.

The full story sketch

One of PowerPoint's limitations is that you only see one chart at the time on your screen. Using the story sketch[4] as a tool allows you to see the entire storyline on one sheet of paper or flip chart at a glance.

The presentation goal (= key question) and the answer, supported by the second level of the pyramid, become your executive summary as we saw in the last section. The statements of the second level are also the headlines of your final charts. So just copy them onto a blank PowerPoint chart. How to best populate them is discussed in the next chapter.

Illustration 24 on the next page explains this approach, showing how pyramids can be put into a presentation flow of sketched charts.

The top half shows the process conceptually and – in parallel – the bottom part shows a very important topic that UNEP (United Nations Environment Programme) deals with.

Most of the time, your presentation will not deal with one straight question. But you can still apply the same straight thinking for creating even very complex presentations. Let's assume you have

Illustration 23: **Converting a pyramid into the executive summary**

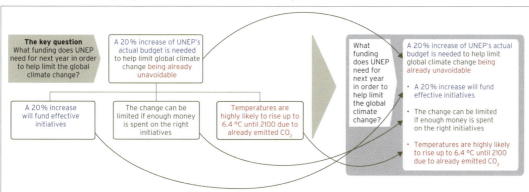

Source: ThinkStoryline!© UNEP

[4] Some call the story sketch also straw man, Mickey Mouse or storyboard.

Illustration 24: **From one pyramid to the presentation sketch**

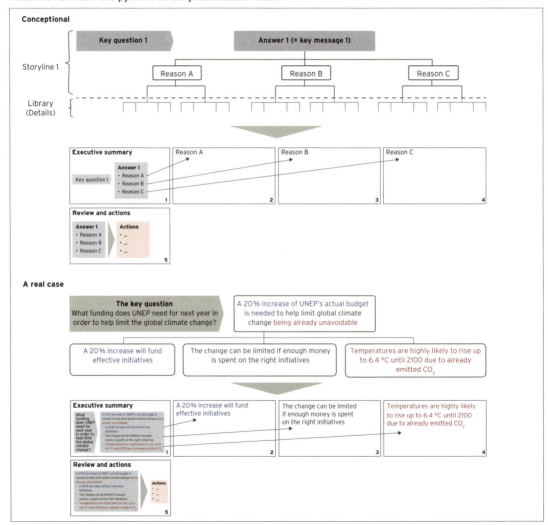

78 ■ 2. CREATE YOUR STORY

Illustration 25: **From two pyramids to the presentation sketch**

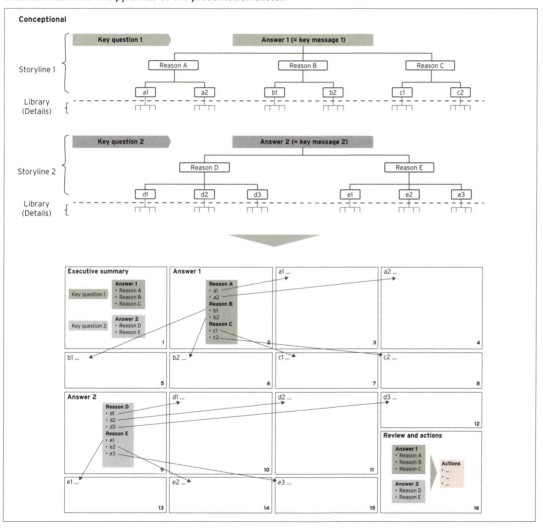

two separate complex questions. All you have to do is creating two pyramids answering each of the questions separately. If the depth of data you need to show is greater than in the example before, just add another level.

Each box of the second level is the "top of a sub-pyramid". Therefore, the statements on the third level support the second level. You see the conversion of the two pyramids into the story sketch in Illustration 25 on the previous page.

The story sketch will prove to be helpful in several ways. Most importantly, you keep the overview about the whole presentation and can share the story with collaborators. You can even divide and conquer the work while everybody knows how his or her part fits into the whole presentation without spending time on PowerPoint charts already. You will also revolutionize the way you build presentation documents. Messages drive the displayed information! In other words: Your PowerPoint charts are only generated AFTER identifying the messages.

At this point, your presentation is almost finished. All you need to do is to find or create the visualization that fits with your messages. How to visualize and make your message convincing will be discussed in the section about visualizing. There you will also find strategies how to use other means of visualization.

The final page: Revisit the key findings and launch the discussion

If you have applied this thinking to your story so far, the last remaining bit is the last page after you have communicated the key question(s), the answer(s) as key messages and the main supporting arguments derived from you second and third level of the pyramid. Most presentations lack a final page where everything is wrapped up. So the audience are left somewhere in the library maze. The way to resurface and to create a powerful last page is to revisit your key messages and the main supporting arguments at the end again. Your audience are on a different knowledge level by now. So they will understand the key messages better and will be ready to discuss the next steps and action points you suggest.

Have a look how the last page of the UNEP presentation may look like.

Illustration 26: **The very last page of the UNEP presentation**

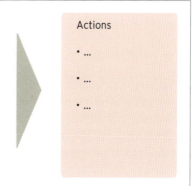

A 20% increase of UNEP's actual budget is needed to help limit global climate change being already unavoidable

- A 20% increase will fund effective initiatives
- The change can be limited if enough money is spent on the right initiatives
- Temperatures are highly likely to rise up to 6.4 °C until 2100 due to already emitted CO_2

Actions

- ...
- ...
- ...

KEY POINTS TO REMEMBER

- Stories stick. Think in stories – not in atoms.

- Little Red Riding Hood contains all elements human beings are looking for in a powerful story: a clear context, introduction of main actor(s) and the task at hand, emotional roller coasters and a (happy) end.

- Consider six story types that are aligned with the FIRE level your audience are on:
  1. Teach – educate
  2. Highlight differences (e.g., actual vs. past)
  3. Create discussion platform
  4. Get buy-in
  5. Obtain approval
  6. Call to action

- Stories frequently have few key messages. These key messages should be supported by logical arguments. The two pyramid structures (group or chain) are very effective tools to structure stories in a logical way.

- Don't hesitate to start your story with the key message at the top of your pyramid in a business presentation.

- The two pyramid types (group or chain) can be used in seven ways:
  1. The top of the pyramid answers the key question your audience have right away
  2. The pyramid structure ensures the logic of your story
  3. The top two levels form the core of your story
  4. You can address challenges early
  5. The top two levels are your executive summary
  6. The top two levels may serve as structure for your table of contents
  7. The statements of your full pyramid can be used as headlines for your charts

- Derive the handwritten story sketch to see your storyline at a glance. Only then plunge into visualizing (or should I say "Death by PowerPoint"?).

- Revisit your key messages and supporting arguments on your last page. This is the perfect setup to launch the discussion about next steps and action points.

2. CREATE YOUR STORY

"We drifted into this [PowerPoint] presentation mode without realizing the cost to the content and to the audience in process." *Edward Tufte*

VISUALIZE YOUR STORY

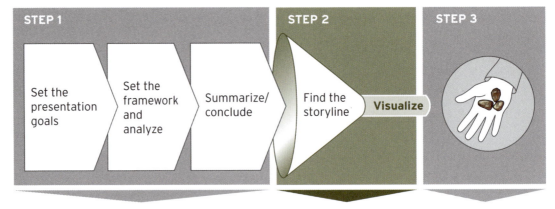

The goal of visualizing is to better embed your story in your audience's mind and to enrich the overall presentation experience. Telling your story with text and images will activate different areas in your audience's brain. You will serve the different preferences for taking in information your audience have. Your story will become stickier.

The primary goals of visualization are simplification and clarification. The human brain is able to absorb massive amounts of information. Based on research, it is estimated that the human optic nerve has a bandwidth capacity of about 10 megabits per second. That is broadband data transfer! Hence, show your audience everything they need to see to be well informed; but not more. Your audience are able to understand high levels of complexity if you communicate them in a clear way. Millions of people browse the stock market tables every day. Stock market tables are not exactly a typical example of simple visualization, but they are clearly structured and consistent. These tables seem to serve their audience well.

Don't hesitate to show linked multi-variant data (for example parameters influencing the weather) or similar serial data (for example sales performance over 5 years in 5 countries) all together if you want to illustrate how they interdepend or may show a common trend. You just have to make sure you allow enough time for selecting the right amount of information for the time slot you have and to find the appropriate visualization (graphs, photographs, cartoons...).

We will now discuss how to best use visualization to bring your story alive in the mind of your audience. There are many tools to project the "film" of your storyline in front of your audience's inner eye. PowerPoint charts are one of very numerous options.

At the end of this chapter you will be tempted to deliver (at least parts of) your story without visual support tools such as PowerPoint charts. You will revolutionize the way you draw charts: by writing down the message first and populating them only afterwards. You will add more visual tools to your repertoire whilst PowerPoint will remain an important one.

A. VISUALIZATION THROUGH YOU

I assume that some of the most memorable speeches you have ever experienced were held without any visual support. Those presenters had visualized their story in their mind's eye so well that listening to their speech was like watching a movie. They didn't need anything more.

I believe that YOU are the most powerful instrument for visualizing your story. Analogies, references to past events your audience can (emotionally) connect with, a logical storyline and your sheer presence may create the filmic experience you are looking to convey. So always consider delivering your story without visual tools at least for parts of your presentation. If you need more, you will find some thoughts about PowerPoint charts and additional tools for visualization in the next two sections.

B. TWELVE ALTERNATIVES TO POWERPOINT CHARTS

Before we go into more detail how to tame the ubiquitous sprawl of PowerPoint charts, I would like to remind you that there is a whole arsenal of alternatives. Let me show you twelve of them.

Illustration 27: 12 alternatives to PowerPoint

1.	YOU
2.	Flip charts (documentation with your mobile's camera)
3.	Metaphors
4.	Known stories (e.g., fairy tales, personal patient / customer story)
5.	Post-it notes, cards with content
6.	Photographs, cartoons (e.g., www.cartoonbank.com)
7.	Articles with questions to answer
8.	Case studies: team / pair exercises
9.	Films (e.g., www.ted.com, www.youtube.com)
10.	Objects, comparisons to items of daily usage
11.	Interactive polls (e.g., www.polleverywhere.com)
12.	Presentation on a canvas (e.g., www.prezi.com)

1. YOU: I mentioned you as the main alternative to PowerPoint charts already. There are many aspects of your story you can tell your audience without any visual support.

2. The flip chart: The multi-purpose star. You can use it to write down the goals, collect expectations or to visualize your overall framework. A flip chart allows you to create a second point of reference in your presentation space. This enables you to move between the computer and the flip chart. Changing your position helps you to interact with the audience more fairly since any position tends to favor one part of the audience.

Once, I helped preparing a workshop that was revolving around seven questions that were answered over the course of a day. The moderator wrote the seven questions onto a flip chart. With this trick, the questions remained visible throughout the workshop and served him as structure to refocus the discussion. He could monitor progress while the seven PowerPoint presentations were used displaying the information needed to discuss the answers. You can also use a flip chart in this way for your agenda or to document the expectations for a meeting.

One more tip: If you develop your line of thought on a flip chart during your presentation, sketch the final picture with a pencil in advance. Your audience won't see it from their seats and wonder whether you are a reincarnation of Picasso at the end.

And don't forget to take a picture with your mobile device. You can then either email it to the participants immediately or create a write-up document without being rushed.

3. Metaphors: You can use metaphors as your "Leitmotiv" in your presentation. Take "A light in a sea of darkness" for example. This may be used when a presenter shows new data for an innovative treatment for a severe disease. A very self-confident presenter may announce that "his presentation would weather the storm of scrutiny". Other very popular metaphors are to talk about "levers", "forces at work" and "clusters". They all allow you to break down complexity into more "visible" chunks.

4. Publicly known and personal stories: Everybody has produced his own movie on famous fairy tales and other well-known stories in his mind. Capitalize on one of them and explain the content of your presentation by using such a story as catalyst. Another way to evoke lively images in your audience's mind is to use a personal story or a real story about a patient, a customer, a role model or another person that links your story to your audience's inner eye.

5. Post-it notes, cards with content: The famous yellow sticky notes are perfect to tease out questions, remarks and thoughts, which would not be shared otherwise because people tend to become less outspoken the larger the audience gets. Cluster them in a break and share the findings with the party in a anonymized manner. Your audience may even have provided you with their thread and you can customize your narrative by going through the clusters of questions or topics you have grouped together. I have also observed that people are much more open to speak up if you prompt them based on what has been written on the post-its. Always leave them the choice whether they want to make a comment or not. This method works well for a silent brainstorming too. This may be especially appropriate if your group is dominated by few, very outspoken people. In this case, some quiet moments may be very productive. Or why not replace a presentation by a card exercise? Ask your audience to form pairs or small groups and provide them with the content on cards. Let them build pyramids where they have to come up with the key insights on the top. It saves you from going through loads of charts in a one-directional way.

6. Photographs, cartoons: A picture may say more than a thousand words. Search the Internet and you may find the right visualization. Even serious business presentations benefit enormously since you make sure that all parts of the brain connect to the presentation content. But I always keep to the rule of comfort: if you feel 1% insecure whether the photograph or cartoon is appropriate, don't show it and keep searching. But don't surrender to the usual "PowerPoint way" too quickly either.

7. Articles and summaries with questions to answer: If your presentation deals with a topic about which articles or even books have been written, use the relevant excerpts as a handout. Let your audience read it, especially if you anticipate your presentation to be a discussion platform or mainly a Q&A session. You may add some questions for individual reflection before you discuss it in the plenary.

We all have experienced that some attendees aren't terribly good at preparing for presentations even if they have received the materials beforehand. Asking your audience to read the document at the beginning of your presentation in silence would mean offending those who have gone through the materials to prepare themselves for the presentation. Letting them read a crisp memo is an elegant way out.

8. Case studies – team/pair exercises: There is nothing more monotonous for a presenter and his or her audience if he or she presents charts for half or even a full day. Provide your audience with exercises like case studies. If you don't want to move them, let them work in pairs or trios. Working in pairs or trios is a great icebreaker too. If you have space and room to move, form teams of up to six. The results can then be presented by the pairs or teams to the group while you temporarily switch to the facilitator role.

9. Films: Many stories have also been told in movies already. Think about using film sequences in your presentation. People connect and may associate your presentation with an event they have lived through in the past. Websites like www.ted.com and www.youtube.com have democratized access to all kinds of clips. You (re)create emotions and your story sticks better. Check it out!

10. Objects, comparisons to items of daily usage: Bring real objects whenever possible. Imagine how dull a product presentation without the product (or the package at least) is. Steve Jobs was a master of this technique. He often made comparisons to items of daily usage. When he presented the ipod nano, he pulled it out from the small pocket within the regular pocket of his jeans to illustrate its tiny size. To put it more generally: Use comparisons to items or concepts for which your audience have a feeling already. It will allow them to calibrate what you present and enable them to place it into a known framework.

11. Interactive polls: Giving your audience a challenge is a very effective tool to activate them by testing their ambition. There are innovative tools like www.polleverywhere.com using the mobile devices of your audience making their thinking visible in real time. Tools like this can be used in many different ways. You can break the ice at the beginning with funny or provocative questions. You can track the learning effect or get the group's opinion. It is a wonderful tool for larger audiences.

12. Presentation on a canvas: Many people are seeking to invent software alternatives to PowerPoint. The next PowerPoint is not in sight yet, but there are interesting inventions like www.prezi.com, a zooming presentation software. Instead of creating a series of slides, you put your content onto a virtual canvas. When presenting, you zoom in and out while moving through your storyline using the elements on the canvas for visualization.

C. VISUALIZATION WITH POWERPOINT CHARTS

PowerPoint remains a most useful and effective tool when it comes to visualizing the content of your story. This chapter explains how you can revolutionize the effect of your charts by applying a few simple ideas.

1. The message in the driving seat

This section will probably trigger your biggest behavioral change. The most effective way to design PowerPoint charts is the opposite of what you are used to.

In the preceding chapter, you have identified the messages of your story. Copying each of the statements in the boxes of the first two to three levels of the pyramid onto separate blank PowerPoint charts gives you the presentation document. I have described the exact process how to do this in the last chapter. The only thing left to accomplish is to populate the chart with the content that is supporting your message in the title. There are two ways for doing that: The chart-first approach and the message-first approach. Let's travel to a place called Utopia to illustrate that.

Let's assume that your audience are the management of a fitness club chain. They are interested in the market potential in Utopia.

Below, on the right, you see a detailed, colorful chart, which I created based on the results I got from "Set the framework and analyze". I only took a closer look AFTER putting the chart together and drew the conclusion "Utopians become lazy". This is called the *chart-driven* approach, which is unfortunately what most people do. It will take your audience quite some time to figure out why you put your statement on top of the chart. The colors are

Illustration 28: **Message-driven** vs. **chart-driven**

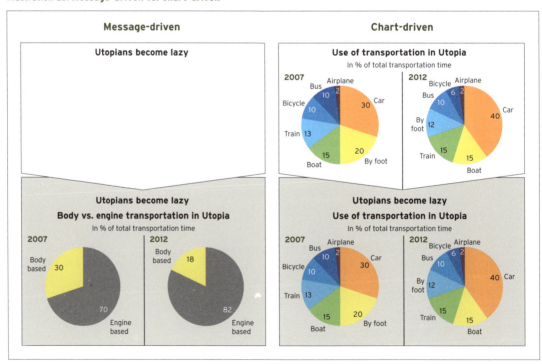

confusing and the two pies contain lots of segments with detailed data not needed to make the point.

On the left hand side, I wrote down what I wanted to say first. I still had to do the entire analysis! But I realized that my message "Utopians become lazy" only requires the display of the decrease of "body based" against the increase of the "engine based" transportation to justify the title. Creating that chart the *message-driven* way took less time than the colorful *chart-driven* version on the right-hand side. The *message-driven* approach is very powerful. However, you have to know exactly who your audience are. You would have to design a different chart on the left-hand side if your audience were the Utopian airport authority instead of fitness club managers. Illustration 29 shows the two basic architecture designs for charts.

The top-down design on the left-hand side is visually more powerful. It delivers the key message first. We instinctively turn our eyes to the top left corner when we read a page. As a consequence, your audience immediately understand what to look for on the chart. Putting the message first also encourages you to start with the message at the top when you present. Many presenters don't present the key message first and lose their audience right away.

This approach also complies with our natural "Z-way" of reading charts. We start top left, then read left to right, then spring back left by going down, read left to right again and so on. This applies to the Western world. I suspect that the natural way Chinese and Arab audiences read charts differs.

Illustration 29: **The two architectural designs for charts**

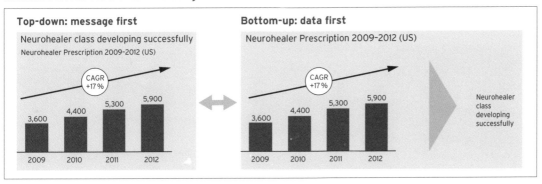

The bottom-up (data-driven) approach is rarely useful. Your audience jump to the message automatically and may not even notice the data.

2. Effective PowerPoint charts follow six rules

Many companies place their logo prominently in the top left corner on every chart. As a rule, we do not notice repetitions after the third time any more and just blank it out. Thus, do not waste one of the most valuable spots on your PowerPoint charts – the top left corner – with logos and similar elements. If you really feel the urge to show your logo, put it at the

Illustration 30: **Effective PowerPoint charts follow six rules**

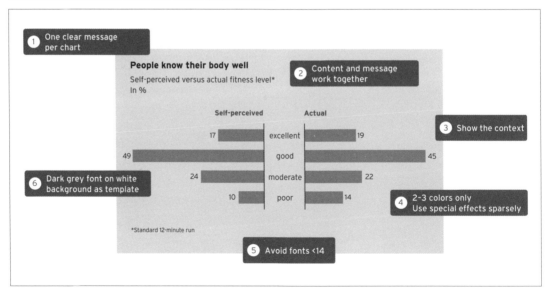

bottom in the middle — as tiny as possible. Make sure that your presentation documents contain page numbers and sources. It facilitates discussions and telephone conferences greatly.

There are a few observations I have made in more than a decade of almost daily PowerPoint exposure. I have distilled my experience into six rules that will result in effective PowerPoint charts.

Rules one to three provide you with guidance ensuring that your visualization enhances the understanding of your messages.

Rules four to six provide you with guidance how to maximize the effect of your visual elements.

Rule ONE. One clear message per chart: This rule is the logical consequence of the approach described in the last chapters. Know what you want to say before you start drawing. The sum of the messages you put as headlines on your charts tells the whole story. I work on my headlines until they fit into one line! This doesn't mean you should avoid complex data on a chart, but do make sure they support only the key message.

Rule TWO. Content and message work together: You can be much more selective and focused on choosing your visual content if you know what you want to say. Show what is needed to support your message. Less is more.

Rule THREE. Show the context: Presenters often assume that their audience are fully aware of the context. So they don't show enough contextual data. For example: On a chart, a lonely line in a diagram rises over a year. This should support "We have had a very successful year". Adding the line for the competitor, the budget or the previous year would help to understand why the year was very successful.

Rule FOUR. Two to three colors only, use special effects sparsely: Our brain is wired to assign signaling power to colors. It has been empirically shown that the use of more than three colors on a PowerPoint chart dilutes a color's signaling effect. The pie charts on p. 90 are good examples. The colors on the right-hand side are hiding the key message, whereas the use of only yellow on the left-hand side enables the reader to understand the message right away.

Special effects like animations are grossly overused. Annoying and patronizing your audience with all kinds of animations is not a good idea. It becomes even funny when your audience are holding a printout of your charts in their hands where all charts are already printed. However, in selected cases, animations can create great effects. Just make sure you rehearse!

Rule FIVE. Avoid fonts <14: As most of your PowerPoint documents serve a double purpose (for documentation and presentation), font 14 is still visible nicely when projected onto a screen. Font 14 allows writing a couple of lines onto a chart without cramming it. I rarely use fonts >24, except for special effects. Messages written with font size 20 allow you to put down a proper sentence without overrunning one line.

Rule SIX. Dark grey font on white background as template: I am a strong advocate of very simple templates with a white background and dark grey font instead of black. The contrast between the white background and the dark grey font is smoother and more comfortable to read. Printing still works fine. Templates with many colors distract the eye and their highlighting power is wasted. Many scientific presentations have a dark blue background with white or even yellow fonts, resulting in an exhaustive read! This has nothing to do with science. It is a mere artifact from the predecessor of PowerPoint charts, diapositives. Their background was usually dark blue to make dust and fingerprints invisible.

3. Two types of PowerPoint charts: data vs. text-driven

The next two sections will explain how you can effectively create the two basic types of PowerPoint charts:
Data-driven or text-driven.
You may be surprised why I don't list bullet-point-driven PowerPoint charts. I find them ineffective and even dangerous. Have a look at one of Edward Tufte's most sarcastic and precise pieces of analysis of a confusing and potentially life threatening text chart on pages 100-101. The chart was used by NASA engineers in preparing for the fatal Challenger space shuttle launch[1].

Data-driven PowerPoint charts
Gene Zelazny[2] found that there are five main message types and their graphs that can be derived from numerical data (Illustration 31).
1. **Component message:** This kind of statement describes a part in the context of a defined whole. Some examples for messages as headlines of a chart are:
    • "We are the market leader by owning 54% of the market."

---

[1] Beautiful Evidence, E. Tufte, Graphics Press USA (2006)
[2] Say it with charts, G. Zelazny, 3rd edition, McGraw-Hill (1996)

- "Cost for raw materials is a third of our total cost base."
- "This product could be used by 4% of the population."

2. **Ranking message:** This kind of statement compares coherent data.
   Some examples for messages as headlines of a chart are:
   - "We have launched the biggest product ever."
   - "We need to double our marketing budget to catch up with the market leader."
   - "Ease of use is key."

3. **Time series message:** This kind of statement shows coherent data over time. Some examples for messages as headlines of a chart are:
   - "We will reach breakeven by 2014."
   - "Our best year ever!"
   - "Will insurance against tornados become more expensive?"

4. **Frequency distribution message:** This kind of statement compares all parts of a whole relative to each other. Some examples for messages as headlines of a chart are:
   - "Customers typically fly with Atlantis Airways twice a year."
   - "The 5-mg tablet is the most popular."

- "Most sales reps make between USD 100 000 and 130 000 per year."

5. **Correlation message:** This kind of statement makes a comparison between two or more sets of coherent data. Some examples for messages as headlines of a chart are:
   - "Rainy days drive umbrella sales."
   - "Carbon Dioxide emissions grow with industrialization."
   - "Hail and harvest are not best friends."

Illustration 31: **Message types and their graphs for data-driven charts**

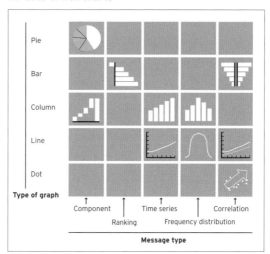

Gene also suggested the matching graph(s) for each of these five message types. You see the five message types applied below.

Isn't that wonderful? From now on, you will know exactly what basic type of graph to choose after you have identified the type of your message.

Illustration 32: **Examples of the 5 message types**

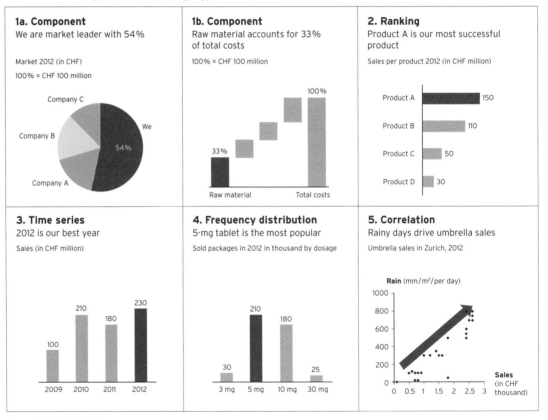

Source: ThinkStoryline!©

Also keep in mind that the x-axis is strongly associated with progression over time. Minimize its use for other types of messages. For example, rankings are often shown from left to right. Show it top-down instead. The gold medal winner doesn't stand on the right of the silver medalist either.

Often, data-driven charts are directly exported from an Excel sheet. This bears some risks. The standard legends generated by Excel are very small, the colors in the boxes barely visible, and the text legend far away from the graph. This forces your audience to go back and forth constantly in order to understand what the graph means. I recommend that you integrate the label into the graph or put an extra textbox next to the graph (see also in the Illustration below). Ensure consistency of color usage; recurring items (e.g., products, companies) should carry the same color throughout the presentation.

Another critical aspect about data-driven charts is presenting series of similar data. Exposing your audience to a series of ten similar charts, which may show the same parameters for ten different countries, for example, is not ideal. PowerPoint's linear structure may be one of the reasons why this happens so often. It is a typical example of unnecessarily separating comparable data, in this case per country, without storylining them. But

Illustration 33: **Audience-friendly legends**

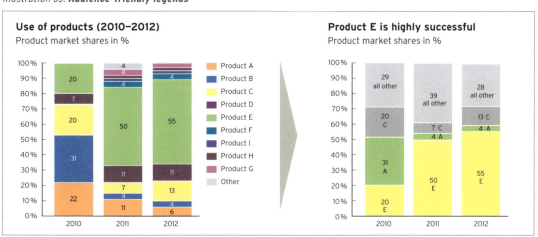

the human brain looks for comparing differences in context, because our mind is not very good at picking up differences if they are not shown next to each other for comparison. Most of the time, you will be able to draw your conclusion from the ten countries by looking at all of them together. You may conclude that the overarching message is a similar trend across countries, except in one. So why not showing this outlier next to the rest?

The two options of overview charts on the right-hand side in Illustration 34 look crowded at first glance. But the data is displayed in a clear and transparent way and the outlier message sticks out immediately. Show your audience everything that is necessary together – as long as you grant enough time and explanation. Remember, neither you nor your audience have become mentally handi-capped. So oversimplification is not required.

Illustration 34: **Displaying comparable information with a common trend**

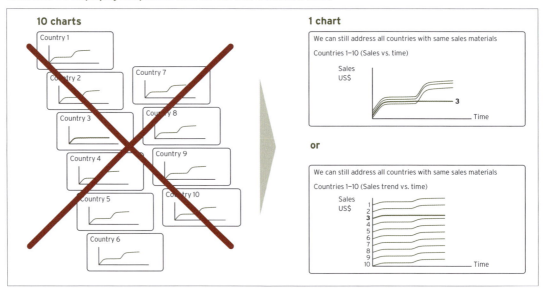

This section would not be complete without recommending the four books by Edward Tufte. He is also described as a modern "Leonardo da Vinci of data". Have a read of or better have a look at his books. They are an enormous source of inspiration how to think about and how to display data. He advocates that PowerPoint is only useful for holding photographs and nothing else. You will probably not entirely agree with him (nor do I).

A final point: Make sure you label every graph you design in a scientific manner, i.e., labeled x- and y-axis, units of measure, type of data, size of sample, sources.

Text-driven PowerPoint charts

Text-driven PowerPoint charts are used very frequently. They often appear to be written like a piece of continuous text interrupted by bullet points. You can improve your text charts by applying pyramid thinking. The main bullet points are your top levels, subbullets the lower levels of the pyramid. You can check the logic of your text chart by asking "why" when you move from the main bullet to the subbullet and so on.

Analytical rigor helps you to eliminate nonessential words – I call them "words for the graveyard" – and ensures that your text is crisp. Avoid buzzwords

Illustration 35: **Applying pyramid thinking to text**

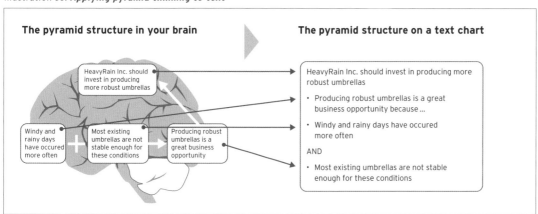

Illustration 36: **Edward Tufte: Analysis of a NASA PowerPoint text chart**[4]

On this one Columbia slide, a PowerPoint festival of bureaucratic hyper-rationalism, 6 different levels of hierarchy are used to display, classify, and arrange 11 phrases:

Level 1   Title of Slide
Level 2   ● Very Big Bullet
Level 3   – big dash
Level 4   ◆ medium-small diamond
Level 5   · tiny bullet
Level 6   ( ) parentheses ending level 5

The analysis begins with the dreaded Executive Summary, with a conclusion presented as a headline: "Test Data Indicates Conservation for Tile Penetration." This turns out to be unmerited reassurance. Executives, at least those who don't want to get fooled, had better read far beyond the title.

The "conservatism" concerns the choice of models used to predict damage. But why, after 112 flights, are foam-debris models being calibrated during a crisis? How can "conservatism" be inferred from a loose comparison of a spreadsheet model and some thin data? Divergent evidence means divergent evidence, not inferential security. Claims of analytic "conservatism" should be viewed with scepticism by presentation consumers. Such claims are often a rhetorical tactic that substitutes verbal fudge factors for quantitative assessments.

As the bullet points march on, the seemingly reassuring headline fades away. Lower-level bullets at the end of the slide undermine the executive summary. This third-level point notes that "Flight condition [that is, the debris hit on the Columbia] is significantly outside of test database." How far outside? The final bullet will tell us.

This fourth-level bullet concluding the slide reports that the debris hitting the Columbia is estimated to be 1920/3 = 640 times larger that data used in the tests of the model! The correct headline should be "Review of Test Data Indicates Irrelevance of Two Models." This is a powerful conclusion, indicating that pre-launch safety standards no longer hold. The original optimistic headline has been eviscerated by the lower-level bullets. Note how close attentive readings can help consumers of presentations evaluate the presenter's reasoning and credibility.

Here "ramp" refers to foam debris (from the bipod ramp) that hit Columbia. Instead of the cryptic "Volume of ramp," say "estimated volume of foam debris that hit the wing." Such clarifying phrases, which may help upper-level executives understand what is going on, are too long to fit in low-resolution bullet outline formats. PP demands a shorthand of acronyms, phrase fragments, clipped jargon, and vague pronoun references in order to get at least some information into the right format.

The Very-Big-Bullet phrase fragment does not seem to make sense. No other VBBs appear in the rest of the slide, so this VBB is not necessary.

Spray On Foam Insulation, a fragment of which caused the hole in the wing

> **Review of Test Data Indic**
>   **Pene**
>
> ● **The existing SOFI on tile te**
>   **was reviewed along with ST**
>   – **Crater overpredicted pe**
>   **significantly**
>   ◆ **Initial penetration to d**
>   Varies with volume/r
>   3cu. In)
>   ◆ **Significant energy is**
>   **to penetrate the relati**
>   Test results do sho
>   and velocity
>   ◆ **Conversely, once tile**
>   **significant damage**
>   Minor variations in to
>   can cause **significan**
>   – **Flight condition is signi**
>   ◆ **Volume of ramp is 192**
>
> *BOEING*

*The Columbia Accident Investigation Board (final report, p. 191) referred to this point about units of measurement: "While such inconsistencies might seem minor, in highly technical fields like aerospace engineering a misplace decimal point or mistake unit of measurement can easily engender inconsis

[4] Beautiful Evidence, E. Tufte, Graphics Press USA (2006)

A model to estimate damage to the tiles protecting flat surfaces of the wing.

Conservatism for Tile
on

a used to create Crater
Southwest Research data
ion of tile coating

ed normal velocity
f projectile (e.g. 200ft/sec. for

ed for the softer SOFI particle
ard tile coating
(it) is possible at sufficient mass

netrated SOFI can cause

rgy (above penetration level)
amage

ly outside of test database
in vs 3 in for test

ies and inaccuracies." The phrase "mistaken unit of measurement" is an
kind veiled reference to a government agency that had crashed $250
ion of spacecraft into Mars because of a mix-up between metric and
-metric units of measurement.

The vigorous but vaguely quantitative words "significant" and "significantly" are used five times on this slide, with meanings ranging from "detectable in a perhaps irrelevant calibration case study" to "difference of 640-fold." The five "significants" cannot refer to statistical significance, for no formal statistical analysis has been done.

Note the analysis is about tile penetration. But what about RCC penetration? As investigators later demonstrated, the foam did not hit the tiles on the wing surface, but instead the delicate reinforced-carbon-carbon (RCC) protecting the wing leading edge. Alert consumers should carefully watch how presenters delineate the scope of their analysis, a profound and sometimes decisive matter.

?

Slideville's low resolution and large type generate space wasting typographic orphans, lonely words dangling on 4 separate lines:

Penetration   significantly   3cu. In   and velocity

The really vague pronoun reference "it" refers to damage to the left wing, which ultimately destroyed Columbia (although the slide here deals with tile, no RCC damage).
Low-resolution presentation formats encourage vague references because there isn't enough space for specific and precise phrases.

The same unit of measurement for volume (cubic inches) is shown in a slightly different way every time
3cu. In   **1920cu in**   **3 cu in**
rather than in clear and tidy exponential form 1920 in^3.
Shakiness in conventions for units of measurement should always provoke concern, as it does in grading the problem sets of sophomore engineering students.* PowerPoint is not good at math and science; here at NASA, engineers are using a presentation tool that apparently makes it difficult to write scientific notation. The pitch-style typography of PP is hopeless for science and engineering, yet this important analysis relied on PP. Technical articles are not published in PP; why then should PP be used for serious technical analysis, such as diagnosing the threat to Columbia?

STEP 2

■ 2. CREATE YOUR STORY

and bullet points with one word only. Your text chart should still be telling a story and not serve exclusively as a reminder for you. Finally, put your text-driven PowerPoint chart under the pillow for at least one night and have another look, since a text-driven chart is never final after writing it down for the first time. Make sure that you don't have to offer the same excuse as Marc Twain had to: "Sorry Sir, I did not have the time to be short."

Concept-driven PowerPoint charts

However, I am still not a big fan of pure bullet point charts. I strongly recommend that you completely eliminate them from your repertoire! There are some simple, quick ways to beef them up significantly. A simple trick to create powerful text-driven charts is to cluster the points and to apply a light graphical structure. Have a look at Illustration 37.

Introducing structuring elements has several advantages for your audience and you. Clustering

Illustration 37: **Alternative to a nonclustered bullet point chart**

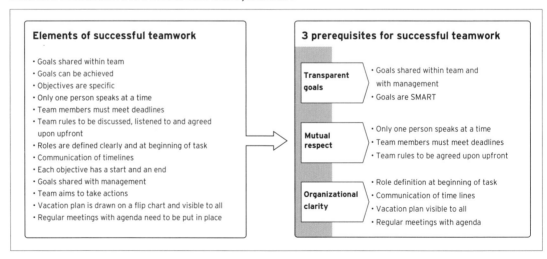

your list of bullet points helps you to identify the key message for the headline. You can present this chart top down in a structured manner without getting lost. And your audience can follow.

In Illustration 37, did you recognize the pyramid structure of the improved slide on the right? The headline is the key message, the three arrows are the first level and the bullet points are the second level. The chart has also become self-explanatory. In case no live presentation takes place, it may even be used in an emailed document – and still be clear.

Illustration 37 is a simple example of better visualizing a list of bullet points with conceptual graphical elements. I recommend visualizing ideas and data whenever possible to address the different reception channels your audience use.

This enhances the understanding of your story greatly. Visual concepts and frameworks are very helpful when it comes to structuring the overall presentation data. Keep in mind that visualization may be the preferred learning style for many in your audience. Visualizing complex messages with one image tends to be much more powerful than a thousand words. Analogies or metaphors may also serve as powerful vehicles to transport your message.

Ideally, your structuring framework tells a story by itself or induces associations. The framework serves as conceptual thread. Illustration 38 on the next page provides you with 12 ideas for frameworks how to visualize your concept. Have a look in what situations I have applied a selection of the 12 frameworks.

The puzzle (1) may serve you as a concept when you tell a story about two parts coming together (e.g., in a merger) and forming a new whole. The notion of a train under full steam (2) could be used for an energizing project kick-off to describe the phases as linked train wagons. If you describe the design of a selection process, filters (3) may be useful. They show the different criteria, applied in order to arrive at the optimal choice. Product positioning might be illustrated as shown under framework 4. The life cycle of a product or aspects of an issue being closely linked to form something rounded may be visualized by framework 5. Promising your audience that they will reach a new level of comprehension can be visualized by number 6. Framework 7 is a useful alternative to an ordinary executive summary. Write down the key questions to be answered and give the answer right away. A common example is market research where mes-

Illustration 38: **Presentation framework ideas**

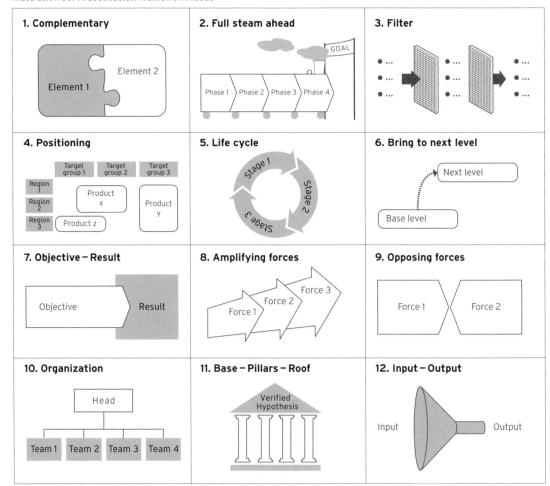

sages, logos or graphical concepts are tested. The audience are mainly interested in which of those made it to the top. This is one example only, but highlighting the essence at the start is appropriate for most situations I have been in. You may want to employ growing arrows (8) for

Illustration 39: **Visualizing messages through concepts**

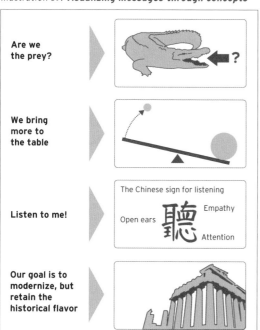

illustrating how to bring a strategy to life. The smallest could symbolize the pilot project, the next the divisional roll-out and the third the company-wide implementation. Framework 9 may be used to symbolize a conflict, number 10 if you want to show what the organizational implications of a restructuring are.

I recently used the temple (11) for a strategy exercise. The roof represented the overarching vision, the pillars the constituencies of the organization and the base the shared values. The funnel (12) is one of the guiding concepts in this book and stands for distilling the information down to the essential storyline.

If you are looking for a more extensive collection of concepts, please turn to the last section of Gene Zelazny's book "Say it with charts"[5]. Illustration 39 shows four metaphoric ideas to visualize messages. PowerPoint as software contains a vast library of shapes. They are quite handy as well.

4. How PowerPoint's limitations can be overcome

It is important that your presentation is not delivered in a linear way, but in a manner that serves the thread of your story best. PowerPoint's linear structure can seduce you to fall into the linear

[5] Say it with charts, G. Zelazny, 3rd edition, McGraw-Hill (1996)

chart-after-chart-after-chart trap! The quickest way to build hierarchy into your charts is to hyperlink your table of contents or your executive summary with the corresponding sections or the library charts to the corresponding chart in the main presentation. Make sure you insert a "back to main presentation" button each time.

With hyperlinked pages, you can selectively present the sections your audience want to focus on instead of feeling obliged to show everything. Your audience contribute to a successful outcome of your presentation by taking some responsibility for what the topic during the presentation should be. A more sophisticated way is to show a pyramid or another overarching framework as "presentation compass". This page serves as the navigation page with hyperlinks to all the sections. Don't forget to insert a "back to navigator page" hyperlink. The illustration on the next page shows an example for such a "presentation compass".

In the middle you see the navigation page acting as the compass for the reader. I took a real case example I did for a pharmaceutical company. The task was to organize lots of data (about 400 pages) into one short document enabling the team of that particular product to access data rapidly. I created the "Business Compass navigation page" first by allocating the data to 10 sections. I then designed 10 charts summarizing the information per section and linked it back to the navigation page. The client then inserted some additional charts into each section, but the document remained well accessible. This provides the reader with a menu to choose from. Senior management might only be interested in the four top sections (executive summary, global sales by product, sales by company, and market shares per region). The junior analyst joining the team may find such a document helpful to get up to speed by reading all 10 sections.

Some presenters choose to hide charts when they deliver their presentation. I am not a fan of this approach. Imagine you provide handouts for your audience and all charts, the hidden ones included, are printed by default. Your audience will be confused because the presentation you deliver on screen is not showing the hidden charts! Your audience have to jump around in their printed handout charts all the time. So keep your main presentation (approximately the three top levels of your pyramid) as one document with the storyline. Put the details in a separate appendix section.

The 12 alternatives to PowerPoint (p. 86) may not replace charts entirely. But think about using them complementarily.

You will find more tips and tricks on how to effectively deliver your story in step 3 (p. 110 ff).

Illustration 40: **Hyperlinked "Business Compass navigation page"**

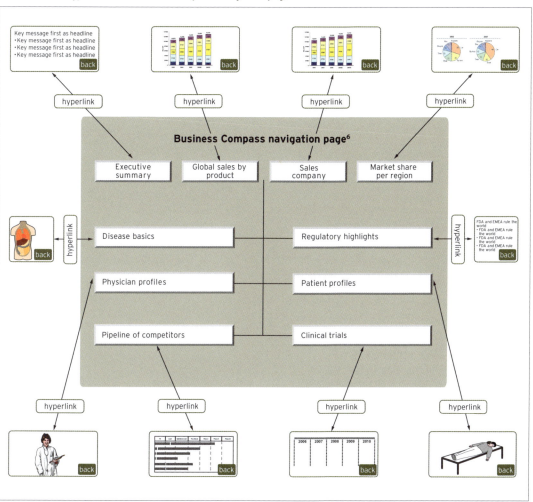

[6] This is the first chart of the presentation

KEY POINTS TO REMEMBER

- Think in filmic stories, not in atoms. Stories stick.

- Try to deliver (at least parts of) your story without visual support tools such as charts.

- Add more visual tools to your repertoire: There are at least 12 alternatives to PowerPoint.

- You will revolutionize the way you design a chart: By writing down the message first and drawing your chart afterwards only.

- Effective PowerPoint charts follow six rules:
    - Rule ONE. One clear message per chart
    - Rule TWO. Content and message work together
    - Rule THREE. Show the context
    - Rule FOUR. 2-3 colors only, use special effects sparsely
    - Rule FIVE. Avoid fonts <14
    - Rule SIX. Dark grey font on white background as template

- Avoid "text only" charts by adding at least some conceptual structure.

- PowerPoint has great features — take advantage of them. But keep in mind that PowerPoint's linear structure is not how we think and not how we tell stories!

3. DELIVER YOUR STORY

"You must feel what you're singing, not just have a good presentation of the language."

Cecilia Bartoli, Italian singer

DELIVER YOUR STORY

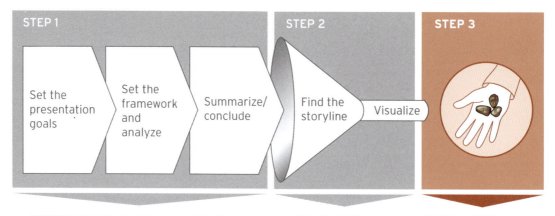

At the end of this chapter, you will be tempted to deliver (at least parts of) your story without visual support tools such as charts. You will be more aware of the different hats you wear during a presentation, ranging from frontal lecturing to facilitating a discussion. Every presentation you give is a dialogue through verbal and nonverbal messages both from you and your audience. Many presenters approach their presentation with a fundamentally wrong assumption: They think that they have to run the whole show uninterruptedly themselves. They hold the belief that they carry the full responsibility for a successful outcome on their own shoulders. The worst thing they can imagine is a moment of silence or a question not exactly complying with their prepared materials. I think that putting oneself under this kind of pressure is unnecessary and wrong. The primary aim of a successful presentation is to serve the audience's needs best and not to patronize or "matronize" them.

Think about the usual behavior of your audience. They are multitasking and not concentrating on one line of thought. Have you seen them flipping through packs of charts while being on the phone just before your presentation? You can celebrate success if you manage to focus them onto your topic during your presentation. You will only achieve this by engaging your audience in a dialogue. Reflect whether you are engaging enough if your audience are still multitasking. Truly engaging your audience could mean a couple of things for you to change; for example, to stop racing through your materials at a speed they can't follow. A successful interaction with your audience could even mean that you pause regularly. Give them and yourself time to reflect, to read through materials, to think about questions and to look into each other's eyes. Such a presentation harmonizes your and your audience's thinking, yields valuable discussions and results with depth. Have you ever heard a symphony with four fast movements played in fortissimo with the same beat all along?

Keeping that in mind, let's now have a look how you deliver your story. But before commencing, make sure that any piece of furniture between you and your audience stays at least a mile away from you. Standing desks are like prisons.

Refrain from dimming the lights in the room! You want to see your audience's faces and your audience may wish to take notes. Dimming the room after the lunch break is especially dangerous. Siesta dreams may supersede your presentation.

The last thing you might want to give some thought to is the room setup. U-shaped seating facilitates interaction and you can move into the middle of your audience.

I like people sitting at a few round tables too. The room gets an atmosphere that is different from an ordinary seminar room where the tables block interaction. People sitting at round tables tend to interact quite naturally. The round table format is my preferred one when I plan exercises in teams. You might even think of removing the tables all together by creating a chairs-in-a-half-circle setup. Your audience should know each other quite well for that chair arrangement. Stay away from it if the topics at hand are very delicate or controversial since the absence of any protection may trigger a great deal of discomfort and defensiveness.

Let's have a look at the actual delivery of your story. Your story needs to be delivered like a play, usually including three parts: the opening, main part and the closing part. The main messages should be repeated. There is a wonderful mnemonic for this: "Tell them what you will tell them, tell them, tell them what you told them." It's like casting three different lights on the main messages if you apply this to the theatre metaphor.

The concept of the "home run" (Illustration 41) will greatly help you to be structured and to provide your audience with the frame to stay oriented. If you have built your story with a pyramid structure, the home run is about repeating the second layer of the pyramid, your main supporting arguments, before you climb back to the top message to close your presentation. The home run is particularly helpful for your audience if you have been delivering a long presentation. Summarizing the data of the main pillars helps your audience to resurface together with you and to be in an optimal position to have an insightful discussion about your story afterwards. The following three sections about the opening, main part and closing shall provide you with some more tips and food for thought.

> **Tip**
> In PowerPoint, hitting the "B" on your keyboard in full screen mode turns your screen black; press any key and you get back to your chart.

Illustration 41: **Presentation delivery circle**

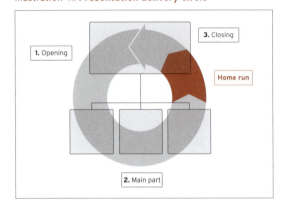

The opening

The start is crucial for you and your audience to connect. Start delivering your story without any visual tools since you want neither yourself nor your audience to be looking at the screen. It's time to get to know fans and sceptics in your audience. Engage them by making eye contact reassuring them that they have made a wise decision to attend your presentation. A good trick to ensure enough eye contact is to task yourself to remember the eye colors of your audience after your presentation.

You have assessed why your audience are attending your presentation by answering question 2 ("What's in it for your audience?") of the four questions when you set your presentation goals. Consider providing your audience with the answer right away. I think that this top-down strategy is the most appropriate in 90% of all business presentations.

I once witnessed a nice example of a powerful opening in a market research presentation. The study tracked whether a product's awareness had increased in the past six months. The presenter happened to know that the awareness increase was directly linked to the bonus of some of the attendees. The presenter showed the increase of the awareness on her first chart. It seemed to be big enough to meet the bonus target. Having answered that potentially delicate question right at the beginning relieved tension and we had a relaxed and fruitful discussion in the next two hours. I have summarized several possible strategies that will activate your audience during the opening in the following section.

- **Release the main messages upfront.** This is much easier if the key message is positive like in the anecdote I just described. But even for controversial news, this strategy works well. There is no gain in repressing bad news. The audience will sense it anyway, especially when they have received a preread document. The "biggest" risk of releasing bad news upfront is that you won't present your storyline as planned, but rather act as a moderator aiming at facilitating a constructive discussion towards improving the situation. A "luxury risk" of releasing the main messages upfront is that the attendees are convinced right away and the presentation closes earlier than expected. Nobody ever complained about meetings finishing ahead of schedule!
- **Ask your audience upfront what questions they would like to have answered at the end of the presentation.** Write those points down on a flip chart and use them as your storyline. Such an opening truly activates your party. And you get additional benefits "for free". You know what your audience's expectations are. You also can gauge the level of agreement among them. By addressing their needs, they automatically take coresponsibility for the presentation. Writing your audience's expectations and questions on a flip chart creates an additional point of spatial reference for you as

presenter. This takes some pressure from you and demonstrates your responsiveness and empathy. Invite the attendees to ask questions during the presentation. This prevents you from patronizing them and you get a sense of what is on their mind during your presentation. If you present updates on any performance, ask your audience to write down their estimate and to share it before revealing the results in your presentation.
- **Put your presentation into a broader context first.** Introduce your overarching presentation framework. It is always good to create some pigeonholes for orientation at the beginning. Placing the specific presentation content in such mental pigeonholes makes it easier for your audience to retain your story. Examples may be to place a given product in the context of its lifecycle or to show the overall strategic goals of a project before sharing the details of the presentation dealing with a specific part of the strategy.
- **Describe the personal benefits for your audience.** Many members of your audience may have rather egocentric goals. I often describe what consequences the presentation might have in the near future or how their lives will become "different" after the presentation.
- **Provide the attendees with the handout before you start your presentation.** Explain how the handout is structured, what it contains and what not. Allow them to leaf through it before you start.
- **Show your audience a chart with the key messages right at the beginning.** Don't bore them with template title pages and generic tables of content.

Main part

The main part provides your audience with all the relevant information in more detail by taking them through the layers of the pyramid. The main part of your presentation supports your main message(s), fosters insight, reassures or paves the way towards decision-making and execution. Keep the promise you made in the opening phase by using your overarching framework and by constantly referring back to your key message(s). If you use an overarching framework, come back to it by showing where you are. Think about what visualization tool is best suited for your purpose.

Introduce your materials before you show them and give your audience time to digest. Lack of pausing and breathing properly between charts and other means of representing information are the main culprits for overwhelming and monotonous presentations.

Point back to what you have said and point forward to what is coming. Keep in mind that your audience see the information for the first time — at least in this context.

Questions during the presentation do not come by chance. I daresay that a significant proportion of them are not motivated by content curiosity, but rather to test the presenter's knowledge. However, your audience might not be aware of that fact and will always pretend to have a more rational reason.

Presentations are on-the-job assessment centers. You know the content to the last detail, your audience — and especially senior management — doesn't[1]. They want to make sure that you are the right person to deal with the topic at hand.

You as presenter may also be a moderator and timekeeper at the same time. You change roles as soon as a question is asked or a discussion starts. Have a look at the box suggesting how to manage questions most effectively.

I always use handouts as a very sensitive tool to monitor how exciting I am. I start worrying if more than two members of the audience are leafing trough the handout while I'm presenting.

The main part of your presentation shows how effective you were when you prelobbied in the planning phase. Your natural allies are those who had the opportunity to give input. You should always strive to include this input to some extent. These "friends" will tend to be supportive recognizing that you have taken their ideas into account. They are your best allies when it comes to tricky Q&As.

The escalating scale to manage questions:
1. Answer only the question posed. Answer with yes or no only if it is a closed question.
2. Rephrase (ideally into a more precise closed question) → get consent from the person asking that you have understood the question correctly → answer it.
3. Use the chart on the screen to elaborate.
4. Include the audience by acting as "ping-pong table": You could say: "May I ask anybody in the audience to express his or her opinion first?" or "That point is not exactly in line with our agreed objective today. Nevertheless, if all of you agree, we may take it on shortly, but we are likely to postpone the last section of my presentation to next week. Is that ok?"
5. Activate hyperlinks to backup chart and go into detail or offer to take it off-line later.

---

[1] At least not up to your level

Home run

Let's now have a look at the crucial moment when lots of presentations end in the middle of an "information jungle".

Let's assume you have just delivered the main part of your storylined presentation. The audience are close to full understanding. The main part of your storylined presentation has been flowing nicely. However, your audience may still be a bit overwhelmed by the amount of information you have presented. Help them to resurface in order to fully grasp the conclusions and to launch an informed discussion by performing a home run. The home run is about repeating the second layer of the pyramid representing your main supporting arguments and climbing back to the top of the pyramid as shown in the presentation delivery circle (p. 112).

But don't say: "A market overview, the competitive situation, the pros and cons of a potential new strategy were presented and thus, we should launch this new product." That is an anonymous buzzword bombardment without any meaning and passion.

Much better is: "We have the glittery opportunity to launch GoldGel because the market potential is attractive, competitors lag behind and breakeven could be reached within two years worth the two million $ marketing investment."

Closing and launching the discussion

Closing is about completing the presentation delivery circle. Do not present any new information when you are closing. Refer back to the opening, the stated goals and the benefits of your presentation. The closing provides you with the opportunity to assess what the effect of your presentation is. So pressing the "B" key (see the box on p. 112) again is essential. It creates the atmosphere and focus you need to move your audience away from the screen towards the discussion on what implications the content of your presentation has.

An elegant way to symbolize the switch of your presentation format is to change your position by moving away from the screen towards the flip chart with the expectations and questions you wrote down in the beginning. Revisiting these expectations may be a good discussion launcher. Get feedback and start the discussion by moving to questions like "If you had to apply this tomorrow, what would you do differently after this presentation?" Give your audience enough space for queries. If that does not work, you can move to a more closed approach by suggesting next steps. You will see how enthusiastic your audience are about embracing them.

Pay attention to the participants even after the "formal" closing of your presentation. Are there question marks left in anybody's eyes? Or facial expressions that need to be addressed bilaterally later on?

Finish on time or earlier! The only time you might allow yourself to extend your time slot is after having obtained broad acceptance from your audience during the presentation. Getting that consent only at the end of the presentation is a farce and no-go.

Please find following some more thoughts and tips in four areas that are closely associated with presentation delivery: body (and) language, setting up the presentation space, interacting with your audience and regular feedback.

Body (and) language

Your body never lies. Your body shows everything you are not saying or you are not even aware of. Most of your body actions will remain outside your conscious realm forever. Thus, I will only present tips you can consciously influence in order to provide your body with the best possible platform. But keep in mind that the most precious aspect about you presenting is your very own unique authenticity. Preserve it throughout any presentation you will ever give.

One of the most frequent phenomena is that presenters speak too fast and without pausing. Their voice is constantly under pressure and never goes down when a phrase ends. Sentences are linked with "and", "hmms", "like" and so on.

An effective remedy is to pause consciously. This allows you and your audience to breathe, to absorb and to think. The only person who might perceive a silent moment of two seconds as eternity is you; your audience surely won't. Your audience will welcome this reflective space.

Keep your hands free and keep them between belly button and nipples. Don't try to control their movements.

There are some no-go areas that are quite easy to control. Hands in your pockets may convey a lazy or overly casual attitude and your body might also appear tilted to one side like a banana. Jiggling keys or loose change are definite distractions to be avoided. Folding your arms in front of your chest creates a barrier between the audience and your body, perhaps suggesting that you want to protect yourself. This happens mostly in the opening phase.

A last word on laser pointers: don't use them. Your hands will do a fine job. Trust your audience being capable to extrapolate what you mean by following your hand's direction. Just allow your audience enough time to follow your fingertips. I have drawn the perfect position relative to the screen and the audience on page 123. Not using laser pointers will also eliminate an indicator that you are nervous. There won't be a red dot quivering on the screen and you won't fidget with the pointer all the time.

Setting up the presentation space
A good golf swing largely depends on the right setup. The same holds true for presentations. The space and the tools have to be prepared in a way that makes you feel comfortable.
Firstly, set up the space the way you like. It should allow you to move. Create points of reference. The screen is one. Complement it with a flip chart where you jot down expectations. Your computer might be another point of reference and the inside of the U-shaped tables another space allowing you to interact with the audience. Remove standing desks.
If your presentation is really important, carry the electronic file on a USB stick to be prepared if you have to use another computer. Your basic position should be on the front half of your feet with your body and hands open towards your audience.

Interacting with your audience
Your main source of energy is your audience. Allow yourself to consume and enjoy that energy early on in your presentation. Little signs like a first smile or nod from somebody in your audience confirm that you are on the right track.
These attendees are also receptive for a first eye contact, which is a powerful connector. Establishing eye contact can sometimes be difficult. If a pair of eyes is further than two meters away, you can look at the tip of the nose of that person only. The person is still under the impression that you look directly in his or her eyes.
Interacting with your audience is greatly facilitated if you activate the party early on. There are some ice-breaking ideas in the section about the opening of a presentation (p. 112).
A well set up presentation space allows you to move and therefore not to neglect any attendee. Don't speak when you move, when you turn your back towards your audience or while you are busy operating your computer. You tend to loose the link with your audience in these moments. Your audience will perceive this temporary disconnect less if you don't speak.
At all cost, avoid putting yourself down with defensive expressions while opening your presentation. Some of the worst expressions are: "I did not have the time to prepare" or "I know that my topic is dry and boring" or "I am aware that my charts are barely readable". Such quotes are an

insult to your audience. Everybody attending is prepared to devote time and interest to you. And no audience come to see a loser. Feel honored and excited that your audience are interested in what you have to say.

Regular feedback

Make sure that you get videotaped every few years. In presentation delivery trainings, I always ask the audience to give feedback first. Usually, only limited input is obtained. So getting feedback from colleagues exclusively is not enough. But you don't need to attend a full-week seminar; just get a professional trainer with a group of colleagues and spend one to two hours individually. Even very experienced presenters will acquire new skills each time and become more self-aware.

A. HOW TO TELL STORIES – THE FOUR FORMULAS

Most of your audiences in today's business world are interested in the (SO) WHAT of a presentation as we have discussed in the last chapter. These can be recommendations, proposed solutions for problems and answers to questions your audience have. You have seen that the top-down formula can be quite effective. The key message representing the top of the pyramid is explained by presenting the main pillars and subpillars it rests on. In most cases, I strongly advocate that a presentation focuses on the top messages and the directly supporting rationale. This should animate the audience enough to ask questions or read the back-up documentation. This approach will shorten monologues and enable your audience to focus on the details they deem important.

However, not every story can be told top down. The key message might be too complex or too offensive to be accepted and understood upfront. Or you might want to keep the suspense until the very end. Budget approval presentations are an example for presentations where a top-down approach might put your audience off. Imagine that you start your presentation by saying that you need 20 percent more marketing budget for next year. Your audience might react to that quite surprised and even aggressively. Chances are that you will talk to a party of shut ears who are not willing to listen to your explanations in an unbiased way anymore.

Apart from the top-down formula, there are three other basic formulas you might consider when you deliver your story:
- The bottom-up formula
- The time formula
- The 3-bullet-point formula

The bottom-up formula

A bottom-up way of telling a story focuses on HOW you have come up with the "SO WHAT".

Most of us have been exposed to this often long-winded approach of telling a story and got used to it. There are two reasons why you should be careful using the bottom-up approach. The challenge with the bottom-up approach is that a long time might be spent on describing the process HOW the SO WHAT was worked out. It may be too long for your audience to stay concentrated. In many cases, your audience have received and read the document already and expect that you as the expert know how to do the work.

However, if you use the bottom-up formula, there is a nice reminder how this is done best. Describe the "Situation" first, then explain the "Complication" and the "Resolution" to finish off. Thus, the above mentioned budget presentation might flow like this:
Situation: "From 2006 until last year, our cost for raw materials increased by only one percent per year."
Complication: "But the situation has changed dramatically for this year. The cost for the same raw materials has increased by 10 percent from January until July already and is likely to surge further."
Resolution: "We need to increase our prices by about 15 % for next year in order to maintain our margin."

The time formula

This approach is another linear approach to storytelling. It starts in the past, then moves to the present and ends with the future. Fairy tales are almost invariably told this way. Have a look at this example:

The king in a once happy kingdom had a big problem with a dragon threatening to devour his whole population. The king promised that anybody who would free his kingdom from this monster would be allowed to marry his very beautiful daughter and be the next king. The daughter was not happy about that since she had fallen in love with the most charming poor student in the world.

A young prince enters the stage. He is wildly determined to win the battle. The battle takes place (the "emotional roller coaster" motive is back) and he decapitates the dragon. He presents the head on a silver plate to the king and reveals to have been acting as the poor student the princess liked so much. The big and happy wedding takes place.

The prince and the relieved princess will be in love forever. We hope for them that no more dragons will ever threaten the kingdom again.

The 3-bullet-point formula

If I get asked a tricky question, I always structure my answer in the following way: "Well, there are three aspects needing consideration." At this point I don't know the answer yet. But I gain time! Having a structure like "3 bullet points" for any answer in mind already helps you to structure your thinking under pressure. You can simply fill the frame without being overwhelmed by the sheer amount of aspects crossing your mind. You can of course choose two or four points too. Experience just taught me that things can often be nicely divided into three. Three as a number plays an important role in storytelling anyway. Plays tend to have three acts, many sonatas and concertos have three movements, and let's not forget the holy triad.

Let's look at an example. A good answer to a hypothetical question like "Where will the value creation come from?" may sound like this: "Let me answer this question by dividing the sources of value creation into the three most important global regions. In Europe, we will see a further trend towards value creation through knowledge workers mainly. Secondly, North America will go into the same direction, but to a proportionally lesser degree. Production of tangible goods will remain important. Efficiency gains will drive the value creation there. And thirdly, Asia will need to act very carefully in order not to destroy value. This part of the world might have abused their environment too much in order to make this incredible progress both in the creation of tangible and intangible value."

In summary, the four formulas (top-down, bottom-up, time, 3-bullet-point) will serve you well while you create and deliver your storylined presentation. In addition, the four formulas are also very practical when it comes to off-the-cuff speeches and to answering questions.

B. DELIVERING POWERPOINT CHARTS

I have observed many great executives who literally regressed to just reading out what was written on their chart as soon as their presentation hit the screen. The magic of their presence vanished, their body language collapsed and they surrendered their entire competency to a set of wordy charts! Let's make sure that YOU direct your charts and NOT the other way around!

PowerPoint is a great tool. Today, it is ubiquitous for many good reasons. However, this format has limitations since PowerPoint seduces many presenters to deliver one chart after the other in a monotonously linear fashion without a thread. But our thinking is not linear. And neither is your storyline, as the pyramid approach shows. Hence, if you overcome this and put yourself back in charge, PowerPoint charts will be a powerful tool in your visual repertoire.

The following seven tricks help you achieving this and make sure that your story and presence convince your audience. You can apply all seven tricks from tomorrow on.

Trick 1: Have a 16-charts-per-page printout ready. It provides you with an overview of the entire presentation at a glance. Keep it in eyesight distance all the time. You know what is coming, thus you can introduce your next chart or interact with the audience with a question before you show the next visual.

Trick 2: PowerPoint lets you access every page in the presentation by entering the pager number followed by "enter" (e.g., "23 enter") in full screen mode. I usually number the key charts of my 16-charts-per-page printout with a thick marker. So I see the page number at one glance. This works especially well if you are guiding your audience with an overarching framework. During the presentation you can click back to that overview page easily, demonstrate progress and keep your audience on the storyline track. Make sure to remember the page where you were last. Just press that page number and "enter", and you are back to where you were. It is one way to overcome PowerPoint's linearity.

Trick 3: Use the "B" key on your keyboard regularly in full screen mode. It turns your screen black[2]. Something amazing happens. The audience look at you and you look at your audience! Furthermore, you will feel how the atmosphere changes in the room and that you are in the driving seat. It is more intimate, more interactive, more human. It is a wonderful technique to start your presentation by presenting the essence of your narrative to your audience[3]. At the same time you can assess how your audience react to the opening. The body never lies. Facial expressions even less. You know who your "enemies" and "friends" are after such an opening. Blackening the screen is also very effective when you interact with your audience during the presentation. You can dedicate your full attention to

---

[2] Press any key and you get back to your chart. On French keyboards, you have to use "N" (for noir) for the black screen, and "B" (for blanc) results in a white screen!

[3] Typically, this will be the first and second layer of your pyramid.

answering the question or facilitating the discussion and feeling the pulse. It also prevents people from still looking at the chart to find more questions. Using the "B" key during presentations also breaks the monotonous rhythm of chart-after-chart and gives you a perfect platform to introduce the next chart without showing it already.

By the way, the **"W"** key turns your screen white – you can do shadow plays.

Trick 4: Start with reading out the title message whenever you show your next chart. By doing so, you comply with what your audience are doing anyway. Your audience tend to look at the top left corner of a chart first (like in a book) and then try to grasp its meaning at a glance by looking at the content of the chart. Remember, title message and content should work together for a good chart. You do this by presenting the title first. You then support it by going through the content of the chart. This approach ensures that you take advantage of the precise wording you crafted when you developed the narrative of your presentation. I frequently observe presenters who wordsmith their message on the presentation delivery spot; the result is that the messages are not precise and do not go with what is shown on the chart on the screen. This leaves your audience confused.

Trick 5: Hyperlink the main presentation to the corresponding details in the backup document. Experience shows that a presentation gets long-winded if too much detail is shown. Provide your audience with the thread of your storyline and let them decide where they need more details. Your audience carries at least 50 % of the responsibility to make the presentation a success.

Trick 6: Don't get caught between your audience and the screen. Move to one side of the screen and face your audience while you work with your chart next to you. You avoid showing your audience your

Illustration 42: **The ideal presentation delivery position**

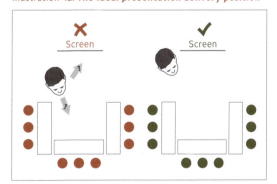

back and you don't look back (and therefore away from your audience) to the screen. It is best to have your base position on the left-hand side from your audience's perspective because you usually present your chart in the reading direction from left to right.

Trick 7: Announce when you are approaching the end of your presentation. Your audience will be grateful. They have the opportunity to get back to the top and put everything into the overall context. Do your "home run" without a chart ("B" key!). You will see where question marks in their faces remain and whether they are ready to take a decision for example. Creating an interactive space instead of a bright-and-busy, charts-on-screen-dominated room is the perfect platform to start the discussion taking you and your audience to the next level.

Ask somebody to videotape your presentation when you apply these tricks. Compare it to an old one. You will be amazed!

C. FORMATS FOR THE SIX STORY TYPES

Your choice of presentation format will heavily depend on the type of story you present and thus the main goal you want to achieve.

I once worked with a client who proudly showed me his short (!) version of his strategy document on 60 pages when we first met. We discussed his presentation goals and found out that his main purpose had not so much to do with the content, but much more with reassuring and motivating his people. This was a "buy-in" story as described on page 125. So we worked for sixteen hours to convert his strategy into a compelling story – easy to remember and inspiring. We ended up with five visuals without a single number! But alas, the client knew his story so well that people were giving him a standing ovation after his inspiring speech.

Think about the great features PowerPoint offers: black key, hyperlinks and direct page access via typing in the page number followed by the "enter" key.

Illustration 43: **Possible formats to deliver the six story types**

Story goal	Audience's FIRE* level	Formats that may be used
1. Teach – educate	**pre** FIRE FIRE	• PowerPoint presentation • Develop material on a flip chart • Provide audience with exercises (in pairs, breakout sessions), use debrief as teaching intervention
2. Highlight differences	FIRE	• PowerPoint presentation • Agree on level of noteworthy change with prospective audience (e.g., 10%) - show only agreed upon differences (e.g., only >10% changes) in presentation
3. Create discussion platform	FIRE	• Provide audience with questions • Provide audience with summary in word and let them run show after reading it - act as facilitator
4. Get buy-in	FIRE	• DO NOT bring a polished deck of charts describing the solution • Bring inspiring material, only few key numbers • Let audience address issues, act as moderator
5. Obtain approval	FIRE	• Bring a coherent deck of charts including all findings, option analyzes and next steps in logical way • Make sure to prelobby in order to know allies and skeptics beforehand
6. Call to action	FIRE	• No charts! Motivate, stress benefits again, provide comparisons, create vision and desire

* **F**undamentals; **I**nsights; **R**eassurance; **E**xecution

D. DELIVERING YOUR STORY IN E-MEETINGS*

More and more often, presentations are no longer delivered in a live setting. E-meetings are used instead. These options can be very effective as long as they aim at procedural progress like discussing facts or sharing information. However, all these electronic formats have severe limitations as soon as matters become more personal. You will rarely succeed in convincing doubtful stakeholders, improving relationships or motivating people. What type of document is most useful to support your e-meeting? If you have incorporated the ideas from steps 1 and 2, the storyline and the number of slides should be appropriate for e-meetings too. Have a look at the following seven suggestions. They will make your e-meeting more productive.

1. **Have clearly defined goals reflected in a storylined document.** Clearly state your goals at the beginning and ensure buy-in by asking the participants for confirmation.
2. **Don't exceed 45 minutes per session – most objectives can be reached within 45 minutes.** Even in live meetings, concentration and focus tend to fade after 45 minutes. This is even more true for e-meetings. Therefore, take a break if you need time and let people dial in again.
3. **Activate your participants right from the beginning.** One of the main challenges in e-meetings is multitasking while "participating". The main reason for this is that the participants don't feel involved and choose to consume selectively. Therefore, you should engage them by asking them to formulate their expectations of the ideal outcome of the meeting and ask questions throughout.
4. **Avoid "reading through" your document.** Just like a live audience, your "e-audience" will switch off if you just read through your slides. One option is to invite people to read and absorb the content first without you presenting. This encourages involvement and sets the stage for an interactive exchange of ideas afterwards.
5. **Be in charge!** Just like live settings, e-meetings require clear guidance. Clearly defined goals and a well-structured document help you to keep your e-meeting on track.
6. **Make interim summaries and wrap up with clearly defined next steps.** Break your e-meeting into digestible chunks. You can use

* webinar, video or telephone conference

theses interim summaries to wrap up the whole e-meeting at the end.

7. **Write short email minutes within 1 hour.** Your interim summaries and the clearly defined next steps form the base for short email minutes. Doing so literally within 1 hour after the e-meeting makes this an easy task since everything is still fresh in your memory. If anything remained unclear for the participants, they too get an opportunity to clarify or provide feedback while the e-meeting is still fresh in their minds.

KEY POINTS TO REMEMBER

- Make sure that YOU direct your charts and NOT the other way around! Use the "B" key.

- Think about using other presentation delivery formats than PowerPoint.

- Take off some of your homemade pressure by having a clear presentation goal appropriate for the time slot you have at your disposal.

- Your audience are your main source of energy. By interacting with them (non-) verbally you make sure they take over half of the responsibility for a successful presentation.

- Remain yourself when you deliver your story.

- Stories can be delivered by using one of four basic formulas:
  - Top-down
  - Time formula
  - Bottom-up
  - 3-bullet-point formula

- When delivering e-meetings, make sure to have clear goals, not to exceed 45 minutes, to activate your audience throughout.

- Use your interim summaries during the meeting to wrap up and to send out minutes within one hour.

SOURCES FOR INSPIRATION

1. The Minto Pyramid Principle: Logic in Writing, Thinking & Problem Solving, B. Minto, Minto Books International, Inc. (2002)
2. Say it with charts, G. Zelazny, 3rd edition, McGraw-Hill (1996)
3. Presentations for Decision Makers, Van Nostrand Reinhold, 3rd edition (1996)
4. Storytelling that moves people, a conversation with screenwriter coach R. McKee, Harvard Business Review (2003)
5. Surprising Studies of Visual Awareness, D. Simons (2003)
6. The power of myth, J. Campbell, Anchor Books, 1st edition (1991)
7. Beyond Bullet Points, C. Atkinson, Microsoft Press (2005)
8. Beautiful Evidence, E. Tufte, Graphics Press USA (2006)
9. The Visual Display of Quantitative Information, E. Tufte, Graphics Press USA (2001)

…and many clients from many industries from all over the world, who constantly inspire me and teach me so many things.

THANK YOU

I would like to thank the following wonderful people who supported me to further develop *ThinkStoryline!* and accompanied me on the exciting journey while writing the second edition: Kathrin Puhan-Henz (my wife with whom I had many hours of fruitful discussions and who expanded *ThinkStoryline!*© to the public arena), Petra England (managing the project and providing input), Horst Pfaff and Marc Aeschbach (patiently converting my at times chaotic PowerPoint and Word manuscript patiently into a beautiful book), my other most valued *ThinkStoryline!* trainer colleagues Raymond Hofmann, Beat Walther and Arjen Iwema (helping *ThinkStoryline!*© to develop into a truly global program), Clau Isenring (a proofreader and native English speaker, compensating for my nondetail orientation and refining the language), Edward Tufte (allowing me to reproduce the «famous» NASA chart), Barbara Minto (the legendary inventor of the pyramid principle), Gene Zelazny (the guru when it comes to charts and sharp, spot-on feedback comments), Truninger AG, and all those who made suggestions allowing helping *ThinkStoryline!* to mature further.

THE AUTOR

Dr. Alexis Puhan (MD) is the founder of skillbuild inc., a training, coaching and consulting company based in Sarnen, Switzerland.

After completing his medical degree, Alexis became a consultant at McKinsey & Company and soon focused on supporting clients with storylining, coaching and facilitating.

ThinkStoryline! aims to provide a pragmatic approach to effective presentation design and delivery. It's suitable for anyone who deals with presentations and loves good stories.

Alexis earned the Diploma in Organizational Psychology from INSEAD and is also an experienced MBTI® Trainer and coach. He is involved in numerous international projects across various sectors, yet, his expertise as a coach and facilitator is regularly requested for healthcare and pharmaceutical assignments.